Inner Bridges is an innovative, channeled book incorporating humor and tips that help you make effective changes in your daily life. Learn the secrets of living a simple and balanced life. Bring peace and harmony into your world.

Earth and all creatures are sadly out of balance. The only way the Earth can be healed is by all humans getting into balance within themselves and with all around them. As this happens, the Earth and the creatures upon it will move into balance. Balance can only be attained by starting with the inner you. This will then allow you to build and cross the bridges between body, mind, and soul, and subsequently, other creatures and the Earth itself.

Hello and welcome to the new world. The new world as you have the ability to make it.

Inner Bridges

Gayle Redfern

Inner Bridges
*Opening your Connection to
Inner Peace & Harmony*

by Gayle Redfern, MA

VPG

Inner Bridges:
Opening your Connection to Inner Peace & Harmony
Published by Virtual Publishing Group, Inc.
ISBN: 1-930916-58-2
Copyright © 2002 by Gayle Redfern
All rights reserved.

This book may not be reproduced, in whole or in part,
in any format whatsoever,
without permission from the author.

Contents

Introduction..1
Philosophy...21
The Environment Connection....................................55
Meditation and Living in Balance..............................95
Using Food for the Connection................................123
Sensory Stimuli...161
The Exercise Connection...189
Family and Social Influence....................................193
Conclusion..205
Appendix I..209
Appendix II...213
Index...219

Introduction

Libraries and bookstores devote special sections to literature written about the inner peace and harmony that is rightfully ours. The readers are one of three categories. One group has already achieved material satisfaction while others believe the personal peace and harmonies are more important. The destruction of our planet seems to interest yet another group of people. Unfortunately, because individuals feel powerless, all they do is complain, hoping someone in control will hear them.

What I discovered though, is that few people understand that our inner focus has a direct effect on the Earth itself. There are people in all three categories who think there is no hope for our planet. I do not believe this to be true.

There is hope for the Earth and hope for all who live upon it. What I have learned through channeled information is that **each and every individual on the Earth Plane has a great deal of power.** Once we understand and accept that **everything** is connected, we will then realize that we indeed can make powerful changes. The one change that is easy and possible is balancing our body, mind and spirit with each other **and** with the region where we live. It is almost impossible to have harmony in one area without other areas receiving benefits.

Because of this interconnection, when we make changes within ourselves, bringing our body, mind and spirit into balance, the results radiate beyond our energy field into everything around us.

I encourage you to consider times in your lives when you have been around either a very positive, loving person or someone who was depressed, angry or hyperactive. How did you feel? The emotions and state of balance of others were transferred to you through an alteration of the energy vibrations around each individual. What do I mean by this?

It has been proven that all life vibrates at a specific rate. When a particular part of our ecosystem is in conflict with its surroundings, vibrating or moving at a different rate, this causes an imbalance. This vibration is not visible to the naked eye. However, we can look at a comparative example, the wind. In a high windstorm, a tree snaps and breaks unless it bends with the direction of the wind. If we try to walk against the wind, we find this movement difficult. This is the same as the vibration. When we try to force a vibration upon our surroundings, there is resistance and something snaps.

For more than two years, through automatic writing and meditation, I received information with two distinct purposes. One purpose emphasizes and explains the importance of getting our personal bodies — physical, mental, and spiritual, — into balance with each other. These are the Inner Bridges of the title. The other focus of the teachings introduced simple methods of achieving this balance.

Inner peace radiates beyond our physical self, bringing harmony to the region around us. Pollution or political strife won't stop immediately but as the peace and harmony spreads, more people will respond, altering their decisions and actions. This is one small way that we can affect the well being of our Earth Plane.

There are two benefits, then of paying attention to our physical, mental and spiritual balance. One is our personal health. The other is the health that we can spread to others through our personal energy field. In this book, we can afford to be selfish and reap the benefits of personal changes, knowing that this will emanate beyond our self.

When anything goes out of balance, the person is opening themselves up for illness or the influence of ego, jealousy, greed. Worrying or coping with illness, aches and pains takes our attention away from the happiness and well-being that is inherent in all of us. Thinking about or fearing negative outcomes breeds negative thoughts and sabotages our spirit.

Brief History

Many have asked how the information came to me. As I said earlier, sometime ago, I started to receive information through dreams and meditations and automatic writing. All the information carried the same theme. The consistent theme was that we, as human beings, **must** get our bodies in balance and be balanced with the universe and nature around where we live. Repeatedly, I was told "2 years." Later, I received the title **"Inner Bridges"** and I realized several factors. A balanced body does not give us a healthy mind, nor does it give us spiritual connectedness and serenity. Balanced minds do not guarantee a balanced, well functioning body nor do they answer the spiritual search so many are after. Similarly, a deeply spiritual person does not necessarily have the body and mind in perfect equilibrium. We must work on each separately and yet together. I also realized that this inner balance radiates to everything surrounding us.

At the same time, I learned that the result of balancing our Body, Mind and Spirit in this dimension, is the gift of moving beyond the third dimension. This transition is not an easy step. However, for our spirit's benefit, moving beyond the third dimension may be the only alternative. There are many different ways that we can move to higher dimensions, some difficult and some easy. Through all the information I have received, balancing our entire being is the easiest, often the only, path we can take.

When it came time to put the information into book form, I asked for help. I was shown a picture of categories, or topics. Hopefully, this makes the reading easier and subsequently the decision to change your way of living. While the entire book is channeled, the sections that came through in trance are printed in *italics*. The grammar in these sections is not always correct but it is transcribed verbatim as it was received. Explanations and additional information are in regular type. **Boldfaced** type is used for emphasis in both channeled and explanatory material.

Who has Given me the Information?

When I talk to friends and acquaintances, they frequently ask who my guides are and who is talking. One day I asked and this is what I was told:

You asked how many of us are talking to you at this time. We are the GROUP of 8 or 8 Masters. We were all with you in physical form when you first learned the teachings. We were also with you at your home that was later destroyed. We have been with you many times. We are here now to help you remember what must be said to your people. They still live in a sheltered world and will not believe much of what you say. Hopefully, we will help you put it in terms that they will understand.

Names are not important but we realize that humans like to attach names so they can develop a sense of their personalities. Therefore, we will give you names. Some of your guides are:

LUKE (Lucas) is helping write the book. He gives you strength and guidance.

ISMURUS, or ISHMA as he likes to be called, is one of your main guides. He is a monk devoted to peace. Ishma calls in the appropriate help when you need it and also helps you develop your sense of humor.

SHAY-LA is here to provide universal love and to help you remember that you can heal simply by touching someone with one hand.

OSMOND is with you to help you help people realize their soul search. You will be able to help people realize why they are on the Earth Plane.

Luke and Ishma have been around me for many years. I am only aware of the other guides when the energy, or tone, shifts during a channeling. All my guides stress their love and desire to help humans on the Earth Plane.

Throughout all the channeling, the spirit energy refers to 'my home.' Over the past 5 years, I have become increasingly aware that I have spent very few lives on the planet Earth. My home is in the Pleiades, a star system on the edge of the galaxy. While I have lived on other planets, most of my learning and lives were spent somewhere in this group of planets.

Often during channeling, I will feel or 'hear' the humor and playfulness of the spirits. I also frequently get the feeling that the spirit world is a wonderful place, filled with humor, gentleness and peace.

A General Message

Hello and welcome to the new world. The new world as you have the ability to make it. We, the spirits, will help you make the changes but it will be mostly your belief in what is right and what must be done. When you came to the Earth, you were each given an assignment. Most of you quickly forgot it and started to drift along with the status quo. You enjoyed the greed when you were surrounded by it. You suffered the sorrow when you were told not to make waves. You followed the advertising and let who wanted to run your countries. "Enjoy it and don't make waves!" Quite a choice. What you did not realize was that each person's assignment involved making waves. It involved challenging those who gave the greed. It involved making people aware that their ego was not always the right answer. Those running governments needed a challenge. Those who suffered poverty and starvation knew, somewhere in their minds that this was not right. Many religions told them it was because of things they had done wrong. If you could only realize that there is no wrong or right in the Universal plane. We have no ego, no emotions, no poverty and no greed. As we will explain later, mistakes were made and all spirits and humans on the Earth Plane have suffered since. We send people to try to help but there are still many that need to be persuaded through the written or spoken word. They are the analysts and they need to look at the information and decide for themselves. They will not accept a 'gut' feeling or 'a little voice.'

Through the egos and greed and misguided motivation, there has been much damage. You as individuals, and as a whole can make changes that will let you discover your purpose and make it easy for you to follow.

*Some of you at this time may be thinking that we could not all have a purpose of saving the world, being leaders. Many of us are simple people with simple ideas. Even people who think this way do have purposes that will help the planet **and** advance the souls' evolution. If you feel that you are meant to be a* *writer, artist or athlete, this is so. These goals will fill in missing parts of your souls' learning. It will also bring about the balance in your planet's life so others will be able to center themselves more readily.*

When you see a painting, do you not feel? When you enter an athletic competition and win, do you not give pleasure to those watching and help them gain some balance? The main difficulty in this, though is that you as a participant will have to work very hard to maintain balance in yourself.

Each person can find the balance and free themselves of ego and greed and this will alter the energy around them. This will spread like the waves in a pond and when there are enough ponds, the Earth and its inhabitants will change.

Right now the waves in the ponds are growing quickly and the vibration in the universe is increasing. For reasons that you will not yet understand, the entire universe is changing. We are here to help you change your small part of it.

The main challenge for each person is to honor your society and family where you are living but make the changes within yourself. No person is wrong. Each person on your planet believes they are doing the right thing. Even robbers and the evils of society believe this. Right is doing the best you can at any split second with the information you have available. Therefore, for them, they are doing the right thing. What each person needs to do now is make changes within themselves and give the information to others so they will want to make the changes.

When they talk about our assignments, many wonder what their assignment entails. What I have learned is that for our soul to evolve, there are specific experiences that we must share. How I like to explain it is that it is like going through school. Each year, we must take different courses. These courses give us new knowledge. So it is with our lives on Earth.

Vibrations of the Earth Plane, the Universe and of course all beings within are increasing their vibrational level very quickly. Much has been written about this quickening and all the changes. People do not realize this or how it will affect them. They are continuing to drift along in the a same manner as they always have and also as their parents. For those who are knowledgeable, they know that changes have to be made to keep up with the children who are arriving on the Earth Plane. They are arriving at a higher dimension. Wouldn't it be awkward if only those few achieved a higher vibration and we had to fill homes with all the old folks who were still driving buggies! This is not necessary. Yes, there will be some on the earth who will refuse to make the changes but others will learn quickly that things are changing and they had better change also. This is why we have asked you to write the information about how beings can alter their diet, lifestyle and environment around them to make the changes.

Some may comment by saying that the genes have to be changed as well and this takes many generations. This is only partially true. If it was being done without all our help, then yes, it would take many generations. There is always spirit guides with planet bound beings but with all these changes, we are trying to bring the planets into alignment with one another. Therefore, more spirits are being assigned to work on each planet. Earth is one of the challenges of the universe. It is interesting that the planet has contained races and cultures who were the most advanced over time but now the Earth Plane is the one of the most backward planets. The advanced races succumbed to the greed and ego that existed on the planet before they arrived.

Remember that greed and ego can satisfy all creatures, if only for a short time. You have in your memory a story about people called Adam and Eve and the temptation. This is the same as the temptation that was fed the advanced cultures when they decided to feed their greed and ego.

You may well ask, if they were so advanced and evolved, having learned that these two were not necessary, why did they succumb? Every once in a while, a weak soul slips through that has not learned the lessons and is allowed to return to the physical being too soon. This happened. Weak begat weak and it wasn't long before this spread and then the impossible happened. People were starting to realize that life was not as peaceful as it was for generations before and they had better change their ways to match those around them. Changing meant developing their ego, feeding their greed, all at the expense of other spirits.

The Universe and the Total are not proud of this mistake and unfortunately they didn't notice it soon enough. They are human! [One of their attempts at humor!]

This mistake is being corrected now and very rapidly. There are the children being born onto your Earth Plane that will have the knowledge needed to bring the world back into balance. There are spirit beings that are working with many more. There are writers who are spreading the word so that people will start to think.

For those beings that are still focused on their physical body, we are offering you information. This is healing the spirit through the back door as it will. Your races are proud of their bodies. They are concerned about how it looks and how it feels. They are aware of the illnesses and viruses that have been introduced. Giving them information that will bring their body into balance with the spirit, the environment and the Universe. This helps the spirits and beings speed up the changes. This will affect 1/3 of the population so they will be ready to meet the children coming to the Earth.

For some time, the Total tried to reach the beings through the churches and the spiritual leaders. This did not work. They were more concerned about the ego and greed. They wanted the most for their church and themselves and of course this included the best material things. The politicians also wanted the biggest and best.

You may feel that you cannot reach as many as you would like but you will be reaching those that the other seeds cannot. We are planting so many seeds that one or more is bound to grow.

The work about their diet should include a daily regime so the peons have something to follow. Don't forget that some people need a simple guideline. Remember to include the overall goal throughout the book. Again people need to be reminded of why they do something. Within the food, you can include step 1, 2, etc. But food should not have a priority over the other categories. Some will go for the exercise before the food. They may feel this is more important for them. Their success will drive future changes.

Just as there is such a thing as the Course in Miracles, *people may start a course in evolution or course in bridging. This is in the future and may not even include you. Wait and see.*

Go back to work!

Introduction to the Importance of Food

Has anybody looked at the eating habits of those who fight others, or let their egos interfere. If they did, they would find that people on the Earth plane become agitated when they don't get the best nutrition and will then pick a fight. Yes, there are other factors but most can be solved by diet. The right diet will leave the body calm and this will allow the spirit to be at rest, or at peace, within itself. The spirit will remember the love that is available to all beings in the universe. They will realize that ego, being the one to get it right is all *unimportant. We are all part of the grand total and all have the same reason for being alive. Everyone's spirit in this Universe is here to exist in peace. This is why they can help other universes when they are in trouble. Yes, there are many Universes besides yours. It is your ego that leads you to think you are alone. Life exists only for the purpose of enjoying the beauty that is around us. This is one reason that the Earth was created. It was given so many beautiful, peaceful parts that it was meant to be available for all beings from any galaxy. What have you done? You have polluted your planet. You have grown the wrong foods. You have developed a way to worship a currency that is not needed. All this because a few beings discovered they could control others. This is a mistake that was made a **long** time ago. All who live today and in years to come have the ability to change this mistake. You can feed your spirit and this will feed the **Total** and then people will be able to live in love and peace. **It is possible and it is coming**. Even though each of you are a small part of the **Total**, you can make a change.*

*Taking care of your body and mind and you can allow your spirit to rest in peace and love and this will become part of the **Total**, that is available to all. Do not think this information is being given to only you. It is being given to many so that we can get beings thinking in terms of love and health. When people are healthy, they can focus their attention on peace and sharing love. We agree that there are many in your planet that do not have the food that you have but it is* *available. When they are shown how to get the balance according to their locale, they, too can get the love that is available.* ***Each locale is given the right nutrients that will provide a balance for the beings who live there.*** *We have shown you how to travel around your planet and yet stay close to a balance. Why do people not do this?*

Your people have to learn to crawl before they can walk. This book must have the basics of the best lifestyle, including foods; then they can learn to walk. In our analogy, walking includes how to travel around your worlds and how to consume foods from other regions. Crawling is simply living in a particular region and eating foods according to that location.

A line in this passage was highlighted because so many humans forget that the diet varies. There is an insatiable urge to impose a diet from one country onto another. For example, people in some parts of the world eat little meat. They do not need meat. Their nutrients come from other sources.

There are many methods or systems practiced in our world today. All, of course, feel their system is the best. This belief is certainly **not** wrong. However, most methods do not include integrating and bridging the three parts of our identity, Body, Mind and Spirit. We also need to look at the amount of local foods that each recommends. As you will see later, eating local food from our region is matching the vibration of the local region with the vibration of our internal body.

Getting the body into balance is a preliminary step towards moving from the third dimension to the fourth and beyond. There are other ways to move but, as we have mentioned before, they are more difficult and slower. When the body is in balance, and at peace, it operates more efficiently. Then we can move our focus to mind and spirit.

Foods and exercise that balance the body are fuel for the mind. They keep the mental energy from running rampant. They keep the sleep calm, allowing sleep-healing.

Surrounding us with peaceful, energizing colors and nature accomplishes the same thing as food and exercise. These four (food, exercise, color and environment) lead us toward a healthy body, calm and productive mind and a connection to a spiritual knowing.

We do know that we have twelve DNA strands and use only four. Healthy bodies and minds leave us open to a spiritual connection that, amongst other benefits, teaches us how to expand our dimensions and our DNA strands. It is important to remember that it is possible to open up ourselves to higher dimensions without increasing our DNA strands or altering the level of our soul. We have had many masters and Gurus in our history who were open to higher dimensions without a change in their DNA. Most were in the fourth dimension. At the time they were on the Earth Plane, they did not need additional DNA. Today, the vibration of the Earth Plane, and all who exist in it, is speeding up. Without the higher dimensions and extra DNA strands, individuals will be left behind. Those who are left behind will feel stress and anger towards society and those who have evolved. The peace of each person and all of the Earth is at risk so there must be change.

I ask you to think of a time in your life when you **did** feel balanced and didn't worry. I am sure you will also remember the love, peace and happiness that also existed at that time. Our reason for existing and living on the Earth Plane is, as well as our personal goals, is to learn to manage emotions and give love to all. These last two are learned so they can be transferred from our soul's knowledge to the knowledge of the universe. For all, **love** is our main purpose for being.

Glossary

Throughout this book, I have used many terms that are accepted in the metaphysical community but not always known beyond. Rather than leave their meanings open to interpretation, I followed the meanings that were included by June Bletzer in *The Donning International Encyclopedic Psychic Dictionary.*[1]

Aura: An invisible, electromagnetic, intelligent energy field completely surrounding an entity, living and non-living.

---

[1] Bletzer, June G. Ph.D., *The Donning International Encyclopedic Psychic Dictionary,* Whitford Press (Division of Schiffer Publishing Ltd.), West Chester, PA, 1986

Chi: An immutable principle in the air needed for life, taken in by breathing; circulating throughout the entire body. (Also known as Qi, Prana, Ki). The energy that is referred to in the book covers more than the CHI. It includes the energy that connects us to the universe and other living beings on this Earth. This includes CHI, vibrational rate, electromagnetic, and the energy of creation.

Chakra: A whirling vortex of concentrated etheric energy, invisibly attached along the spine from the base to above the head. The main seven are:

1. Root (base of spine)
2. Spleen (also known as sex and emotional chakra, just below navel in pubic area)
3. Solar Plexus (hollow between lower ribs)
4. Heart (center of chest)
5. Throat (center of throat)
6. Brow (also known as "third eye;" between the eyebrows)
7. Crown, (crown of head)

Dimension: term used by authoritative metaphysicians who grouped the varying vibrational frequencies into seven different states of matter. 1st is linear, 2nd is moving back and forth, flat, 3rd is moving with height, width and depth, up, down, back and forth, 4th dimension is time and space.

While the following material covers areas of health and well-being, it is important to remember that each of these helps us move into balance and build connecting bridges between **Body, Mind, and Spirit.** This balance and connection moves us to higher vibrations and new dimensions of life.

As you read the following chapters, it is important that you understand that you are being taken on a circular trip, crossing many bridges connecting Body, Mind and Spirit. The chapters for this trip are:

1: **Philosophy,** explains the principles and basic understanding of why it is important to use local energy and products.

2: **Environment.** Since no individual stands alone, this chapter shows us how our external environment is bridged to all three aspects of ourselves, body-mind-soul.

3: **Meditation** is perhaps the most important chapter for bringing inner peace and balance to our spirit and mind. It must be used in combination with other chapters.

4: **Food** is one of the simplest methods of balancing our entire being. While it is the strongest, the next four are good alternatives or additions.

5: **Sensory Stimuli.** We tend to ignore the impact of all sensory information on our total being.

6: **Exercise.** Physical exercise helps all three parts of our inner being. This section is small but *very* important.

7: **Family and Social Influence.** Understanding this influence helps us learn how to use them to our benefit or when we need extra tools to counteract their imbalance.

I have included several poems or quotations that came at various times through the writing. It is interesting to observe that all include the elements of life. They are reminders that we are not alone and we should also honor spirituality that connects us to these elements.

Follow the wind, it gives you freedom
Follow the Earth, it gives you stability
Follow the water, it gives you cleanliness
Follow the air, it gives you creativity
Follow the fire, it gives you joy.

Read on. I encourage you to enjoy yourself, and to absorb what is relevant and leave the remainder for another time.

Philosophy

Inner Bridges encompasses a very simple philosophy. Whenever possible **consume** from the region where you live. **Balance** your internal Body, Mind and Spirit and align with the environment, stay **centered**, **give** as much as possible to the rest of the world, and take only what you **require**.

Living is meant to be simple and beautiful. The Universal beings live simply and peacefully. It is only because we choose to live as humans with emotions and egos that we forget this. Many will argue that their lives are certainly not simple, nor are they beautiful. This is when it is time to remember that we, as individuals, always have a choice. We can choose to embrace our emotions and live an exciting life on a roller coaster. We can choose to live a sedentary life with no emotions but still have an exciting and beautiful life. It is important to remember that the only thing that we **really** have control over is ourselves. We are free to choose our own path. This chosen path does have a profound impact upon environment and those around us. I can hear many muttering that they want the ideal life and they also want the world to improve. But, they are stuck with the echo from their past saying that one person cannot make a big difference and each of us should make their life exciting, it is the only life they will live. In the Introduction we talked about how the energy of one person impacts their surroundings. When we are at peace, all the beings around us will be at peace. Simplicity is only one step to this peace and simple does not have to be boring. It is boring only when we choose to make it boring.

Elsewhere in this book you will see the pieces of information passed to us that talk about 1) **peace & integrity,** 2) **eating locally,** 3) **living simply and** 4) **giving thanks.** None of these ideas are new. They may be new in this combination but they are not new. Combining the four gives us a life that is far from boring.

Peace is a misunderstood word because of overuse. We are talking about peace for the individual, not peace amongst mankind. However, when the person enjoys personal peace, the second will automatically follow. Peace for the person is not achievable without the integrity of being true to personal values. Even someone who has committed atrocities has personal values. These values, unfortunately, may be self-serving and filled with ego. This does not generate integrity.

Integrity comes from giving the best we can to ourselves and all around us; all given with love.

Eating locally is one of the main features of the information that has been passed to us. We must align the energy of our body with the energy of the Earth. The fastest way is to start at the closest point of connection. This is the Earth immediately around us. It is not the Earth feeding plants 5,000 miles away. The faster we can align, the faster we can receive information from the Earth and other beings and the faster we can heal our body.

A **simple life** also does not mean that it is not without laughter and play. Both of these are part of the joy of living this lifetime as a human. Once we understand the necessity of laughter and play, we can learn how to use them to enrich our lives. Then and only then, can we store this knowledge in our cellular memory. This allows us to transfer the gifts of laughter and play to the spirit level of our being to be shared by all beings in the universe. We all have access to information of the Total.

All living things, from single cell beings to the most complex are on Earth for a reason. When we take that life away, we interfere with that purpose and with the plans of the universe. This is why **giving thanks** is so important. When we ask permission and give thanks, we are honoring the integrity of all living. We are not assuming superiority of ourselves, which would only reflect our egos.

Our inner bridges spans these four and connect our body (2 and 3) with our mind (4) and with our spirit (1). It is only when we have bridged the being that goes by our name, that we will be able to move upward and climb the bridge from one dimension to another.

This section contains the channeled information that supports the reasons for peace and integrity and the rationale for following the other steps in the following chapters. As mentioned in the introduction, the main guide energy called itself LUKE.

Love is what will open the door for people to see the need. When love spreads, they will be willing to hear, listen and help. You will know the ones that love sufficiently to help and will know how to get the information out.

Love is such a short supply commodity and yet it is such a simple one to provide. It is one of the best ways to balance internal energy. People will someday understand.

Pride is one emotion that will help people spring into action. It will be pride in themselves and pride in their environment. When people realize that they can no longer be the person they desire or the environment is no longer desirable according to their perception, they will be changed. In time you will be shown the way to tap into this pride. It will be the key to making people understand and wake up.

Pride is not to be confused with **ego**. Pride can be used for the good of all. Ego is for the good of the individual.

Stand up aggressively for the truth. Aggressive does not mean violently or arrogant. Rather it means strong and stately. When someone appears stately/regal and confident it says a lot more than an aggressive position. When you look at flags flaying you will see a stateliness, almost regal. People respect that.

When you look at your truth, ask yourself. Is it the universal truth? Very often individuals will pollute the universal truth with a desire to make the truth suit only them. There are people in your world today that *have come from other times that have polluted the truth to their own end. They are with you today trying to persuade the same souls that there is the right way. It is important that when you stand up for your truth that people will believe. It doesn't matter that people begin to believe the information but rather that they know you believe. When they see one person believing in their own truth, they will stop and question what they are believing. If it is a polluted truth, they may question you and believe their own all the more. This is why people must learn to follow their **gut** truth. They must see the peace that you have found and they will learn that their own **gut** truth will also bring peace.*

*A regal aggression is a soft aggression. It is spoken in a mild manner and tone. People will realize that you do not "care" whether they follow your truth. This is what happened 2,000 years ago. People wanted to have people follow their truth and they polluted the truth that was around. It forced people to stray away from their own personal truth and begin to believe another false truth. The truth was not necessarily false since it was the truth for **one** person.*

*When people started to stray from their own truth, they started to get sick. Disease started to follow. Today, so many people are not following their own truth and sometimes not even others, that it is not surprising that disease is rampant in your world. When people start to believe, this can change. It is important that they let go of arrogance and follow a simple truth. When you ask yourself "Is this action for the good of **all** mankind including myself?" When you* *can answer yes without your **gut** responding, then and only then, will you be speaking the universal truth. Many people believe they are following the truth they believe is universal, such as churches that are around today. However, the difference is churches are not truly working toward a universal truth. Example: A church says you should give a certain amount of money, tithing, to the church. This means that you may not have sufficient for your family or you will be unable to help someone you meet. Is it not better to give to an individual that you meet personally rather give to an organization that will apply only a portion of your money to helping others? Another example: you follow a policy set by a church and criticize other churches for not having the **"real"** truth. How did one church get the real truth and not another? Each individual in both churches will have a personal universal truth that is balanced within the universal truth. By maintaining this individual truth, we are able to maintain a balance of the universe without illness, arrogance. Humility and peace will prevail. Be like the heron and only act aggressively when stating or standing up for your truth.*

    Islands. *Most of you look at islands as a safe, secure haven that you can go to avoid other people, issues and crowds. Have you not realized that all islands are connected? This applies to islands of land, islands of people, continents, islands in space, all islands. All you have to do is take a risk and wade over to the next island. There you will find answers to your problems, people of similar ideas and simple* *ways to share. No one person or thing should, or can, try to live alone. Each and every living thing needs something or someone else to survive. An isolated "island" of your body must have a connection to other parts. Look at your history and the Hawaiian Islands. The Polynesians thought they were alone in your world. However, when trouble came, they dared to risk getting their feet wet and moved beyond the horizon to seek out help in the form of the new life. So it is with your people, you like to think of yourselves as the only intelligent creature in the world and universe. You are trying to solve all your problems alone. Yet, simply by calling for help from other worlds and guides, all your issues can be solved. There would be cures for all your illnesses, secrets for getting along so there would be no more wars.*

What is the point of life?

Life is a daisy. Life is a pansy. Life is meeting people. Life is getting new experiences to take forward with us. Life is the joy of seeing a new flower a new leaf. It is the joy of making someone happy. Living is not meant to be depressing, painful, sad or hard work. When you look at a daisy, what do you see? A happy face with plenty of choices. A pansy allows you to be free and move with the wind. Each life has all the freedom it needs. It is only your society that put restrictions on each person. Each person has choices in his/her life. It is how they make the choices that is what gives life a purpose. We need to move forward, forgetting past bad experiences. All too often we see people become afraid to live. They remember *experiences that did not appear to be the best choice. It was the best choice for that time but it is important to remember that every time you have a choice to make, you are a different person in a different time. Ask what makes you happy. What do you **really** want and then go for it. With this in mind and knowing you are not hurting any one, the choice will be the right one. It may appear that the choice means you have to struggle for a while but when happiness and fulfillment comes out of it, then the choice is the right one.*

If you still doubt a decision, ask yourself what the answer would be if you pulled a daisy?

Disappointment. *When someone on your Earth Plane is disappointed, they tend to forget the universal picture of their life. They are so caught up in the minute. You have much to offer and you should work with young people to help them realize that disappointment comes from too high expectation. By all means strive for the most but realize that all of you on the planet are babies. You must take the first step and hold someone's hand before you can run. When you talk to someone who is starting a new project, you may loan one of us because we are capable of being in more than one place at any one time. Even though I/we are in your etheric belt so that you can talk to us, we are still dealing with other energies all over the universe. Your new world is much like the old one since there is no change between old and new..we and they are all one. Your people must realize that the world is at your feet to use for healing, feeding and all you have to do is ask.*

*When you use anything, stone, flower, ask permission and do it with thanks. Even when you get something that has passed through many hands, you can still ask permission and give thanks. The core being will remember and will appreciate. An example that might clarify this thought is new clothing. It has passed through the farmer, the processor from fluff to wool or cotton, to the mill where the material is made, to the factory, to the freight, to the store and to you. The inner essence is **not** destroyed. Each time the original piece is broken apart, the essence will subdivide.*

In another piece of channeled information, we were reminded that everything that happens to each cell in the universe affects the entire universe since the memory is one. A disappointment to one individual is minuscule to the entire population. However, how we handle that disappointment affects the whole. When we get caught up in the immediate, we are slowing down and perhaps changing the process of someone far from our intimate world.

When they talk about essences they are referring to the essence or energy identity of living things such as plants. The essence is received by putting the flower or stone into pure water and allowing the energy of the sun to transfer the energy into the water. The same source can be used to generate many containers of water and essence energy.

When guides spoke about the original piece being broken apart, it is important to understand that the essence and knowledge stays intact. Our human body works in a similar way. When an arm is severed, the identity or character of the person does not disappear or change. It is stored in each cell.

*Patience is one of the hardest traits to learn and accept. Compassion is closely behind. However, compassion has a bit of ego involved. Patience is blended with love, especially of those you love. Not all humans have the same lessons to learn in this life. It is important to be patient and not try to push them into lessons of older souls. When someone does not understand where you are at, ask us for help in determining whether they need something explained or just know when to close your knowledge into your inner self. There are times when patience can be learned **and used** with the teaching. Other times it is for patience in knowing that the person will never get an understanding of where you are.*

Life is as simple as you choose to make it. *It you try to explain something to a person who is not ready, you get frustrated and can become ill. When you try to explain to someone who chooses not to understand, you can develop a hatred and intolerance which will make you an unhappy person and make you judgmental. Judgment is something that is better left to the inner being or the higher soul. All beings on this plane (earth) are not meant to judge. All have something to learn and all have something to offer.*

If you find it frustrating, be assured that if they are meant to learn it in this life, they will soon discover it and they will be able to rest and revel in the glory of discovery, a marvelous thing.

Many will argue that compassion contains ego. Many will also maintain that compassion and altruism are very close in emotions. Some insist that neither truly exists. I personally do not believe this. I feel that compassion and altruism are the purist forms of love that we can extend to all living things.

*When you want something bad enough, it is often the most difficult thing to achieve and yet the easiest. This is because your concentration can be focused. Have you ever thought about how great your life could be if you made a decision to concentrate on things that would bring comfort and perhaps pleasure to mankind and the earth **and** all other beings. Your race spends so much time concentrating on getting things that bring pleasure, forgetting that the most pleasure can be achieved through bringing happiness to those around.*

*It is important to have people realize that they **must** give what is wanted or what is in the other's best interest. The natives all over the world honor life and when it has to be taken, ask permission. This should be done with all humans. Can you imagine the scene where a person on a bus, stopped and asked permission for kicking someone out of a seat, or a robber asking permission before robbing. I wonder what would happen! Apart from wonder and judgmental thoughts, I suspect there would be a more gentle thoughts about the robber and how unnecessary the belongings really are! This is what we were referring to when we said the most needed are often the most difficult and yet the easiest. It is hard to* *concentrate on something that is hard to achieve but since it leads towards your soul's purpose, it is the easiest. Climbing a mountain is hard but it is easiest when you know that you will have a view at top or know that you are the first.*

*Tonight you looked at the stars. It is possible to reach **each** one of them. What you find on the stars will do what you expect. This is because your thoughts will direct you towards the best star for you at that particular time.*

*What turns people off their path? Greed is the easiest way. That is no effort. **Not** honoring fellow humans and all life. We doubt very much if your society would take time to ask for forgiveness each time they walked on the earth or built a new machine. But we hope this will happen. As the new world and new knowledge grows, this may happen more often. It is important that people slow down and when they do slow down, they'll have the time to honor and ask permission. Unfortunately, it will not happen while you are living on the earth. When you return home, you will be able to see this happen from afar. A major disaster may, and most likely, be the only way for people to slow down and realize the damage they are doing to everyone concerned.*

Editing and change are two of the most useful practices of life, all life. We need to develop a fine division between the reviewing and editing of what we have done without the commonly called habit of re-hashing. All of your people should review what has gone before, look at it, decide if it could have been done differently and then make a promise to yourself that should the event occur again, you will change. You have the privilege of being able to change and that is how you grow. Even if a person is not on their chosen life path, they can change what they do in response to different occasions and that will help meet their life purpose.

Life is an illusion or a mirage. How you respond to this illusion is what your happiness depends upon. Many people try to become the illusion and are very unhappy when this does not work. Others try to ignore the illusion and they are left feeling that they should be completing something that has not happened.

The best response to an illusion or an mirage is to ask yourself, "What is it there to teach me?" Most illusions are like dreams. It is only one more method that we have of drawing your attention to what is important in your life. A mirage or illusion may be something to chase or it may be a picture of what is possible. All things are possible and you have only to ask yourself — "How can I achieve it and what it will accomplish towards my life's agenda?"

Time. *Time in your world is something that people spend energy worrying about. As you know, time is of no importance since everything is moving at the same time. Past is present is future. However, you must realize that time **is** running out as your people see it. They are discovering that there is less of a difference between present and future. Your world is changing. Your roles are changing. Your people are changing. For all of you this can be a very unsettling period.*

*Take a simple example. Today you wake up with two legs and hair. If, according to your time, you woke up this tomorrow and had **no** legs and no hair. This would be OK in the evolution of time but you would need to adjust and your people would not be able to. If adaptation came as quickly, you would know that you don't need feet to move around and hair does not offer protection against the cold and heat.*

To Spirits who are sent to the earth to experience time and a slower experience, this would be upsetting. What would the spirits on the Earth Plane do about this? Humans can follow the same practices.

1. Learn to trust what happens and not block it. Everything that happens is for a reason. Yes, for mundane situations, there is a choice but for bigger situations and lessons, they must be accepted as it appears.

2. Look around you and take a minute to see what is present and what you can do to keep it as is. You are building a small wall between past and present that will keep present separate from future.

3. Say no to changes that people try to make unless you can see a strong reason for it that will help the world and all present and future spirits that choose to live in the Earth Plane.

*4. Ask yourself **why, why, why?** Opponents will have the answer to the first **why** but are seldom prepared for the second and third. Have you ever observed a child who continually asks. They are still between worlds and trying to understand the strangeness. Usually the first why does not give them* *a satisfactory answer. Next time a child asks, and repeats, question yourself.*

This is putting Time in the context of our world. In the great scheme, time does not exist. We just are.

They also talk about choices. Many do not feel they have a choice. However, this goes back to the assignments we take on when our soul comes to Earth. We may have agreed to complete something but once upon Earth, we may not like the players or the circumstances. We can always choose to wait until another life. There are many books written on these subjects.

Peace comes in bubbles. *When people first hear this, their reaction is that bubbles burst, therefore peace is never lasting. That is not so. Bubbles can be as strong as a spirit, country or race wants. When there is peace in a bubble, it gets stronger and grows bigger. Gold and green bubbles around your home, and as many other places as you can put them, will help to spread peace in the world. On a peace day, have many people blow bubbles into the universe to help bring peace to all species. At a funeral when people are saying good-bye to a spirit, blowing bubbles is a way of sending peace with that person. People who lose a loved one will bring peace to themselves and the departed by blowing bubbles and releasing them into space. Again, a picture will remind people to blow bubbles.*

*We said that **peace** comes in bubbles and bubbles pop. They are, in fact, very easy to pop. What your people must realize is that a bubble must be coddled,* *held gently and filled with peace and love. It is not something to toss about like a basketball.*

The arrowhead is a symbol used by races around the universe. It is one of your own symbols. It represents peace, strength and healing. There should be a strand of arrowheads around the neck for self-healing all the time. For you, it should be the universal colors.

To heal the entire body of allergies, an arrowhead pointing to the sky will send all allergies to the ethers, heal the home and those in it. It does take time, a couple of months in your world but it will work. In the meantime, those with allergies should not take chemicals but concentrate on foods to balance the body and help get rid of the unwanted chemicals in the body. If, possible, an arrowhead in each room, especially where you sleep will help. For sleep, green and soft pink are the colors to put in the arrowhead.

Balance and energy of the earth, universe and ourselves is interconnected. We cannot have one without the others. As soon as we deny the existence of anything else, we deny ourselves. These are important premise of life itself. All messages from the Universe, Ascended Masters and religion break down to these basic concepts. It also reminds us that we are light. When we first look at ourselves we see a light being but this is only because our energy expands to the form of the being that is looking. We are or can be as small a spark of light or as big as is necessary.

When the wind blows, it will blow as strong as the people need to receive. Most people will perceive it to be a gentle breeze but a few will complain that the wind is too strong. This is the same with life. Most look at life with a good approach but those who choose to complain will complain no matter what happens. It is important to understand that they will not be helped. If you tried to help them fix one problem, they will find another. Do not get caught up in their games and issues. Send love but focus more on your own growth and path. Your path is always good. Each person or soul came to earth to experience lessons. Some of them will be considered a challenge but if they look at these challenges, they will realize that the wind is gentle. This is not something that you can teach or tell people, it is only how they look at life. When people realize that all is for the best and each person comes into your life as a mirror or teacher, then they will see the wind as blowing gently. When you identify a mirror, rather than just observing, ask what it is that irritates you about them and most likely this will be the mirror. They cannot simply enjoy the experience. They must be a teacher. So it is sometimes with yourself. Always stop and enjoy the view.

When you interact with another, record the main issues after and then you will see what the mirror is telling you. If you notice a trend, then you can look at yourself and decide what and if you want to change. Remember the reverse image of mirrors. All souls that are on the Earth Plane must learn to balance both these sides of their personality. In spirit, we have both sides and as a guide, we must learn how to balance them. People on the Earth Plane do not always appreciate a playful, silly guide. This is what they dismiss as useless. They do need it, however.

One reason you enjoy the clouds so much is that the wind is showing a playful side as well as the serious. You can look at the softness and see the playful. Clouds are the only way that mankind can see the currents and aspects of the wind. It is like putting color on paper so that you can see an image.

Energy should be lined up like focusing a camera. If the lines are not uniform, the picture is blurry So it is with the energy of the earth, universe and body; all must be lined up.

Sorrow is not something that you can ignore nor change. It is something that is placed with you to balance karma. When someone hurts you, it is most often because of karma in a past life. It is not important to understand what happened. Rather it is better to accept and move on. If someone is grieving, it will cause a blockage in the host body and prevent a fulfillment of the life purpose. It is better to shrug and move on.

People are not put on the earth to please others. They are on the earth to meet their needs. You may say that this is very selfish. It is. In many ways the soul is very selfish. It is only by fulfilling the soul's needs, that the needs of the whole can be fulfilled. However, if forgiveness is not asked for or given, a karmic lesson will be harbored until a future life and the cycle will never end. Asking forgiveness, even when it is not clear what for and / or giving it is one of the greatest rewards and joys in life. There is always time and the right time to forgive

By standing alone, you are able to fulfill your life purpose. It is necessary to remember that your purpose is yours alone, not others. It is important to recognize this and accept responsibility and move on. Others may help but only if they want to. Most people will not understand your purpose and will be busy working on their own. A life purpose is usually a lonely life.

"Right to Die" or Euthanasia, *as you call it. Yes, people do have the right to chose their time of death. However, it must be remembered that a soul is not on the Earth for its purpose only. If a soul decides to die at a certain time, it may create karma (as you call it) or it may truly be the best time. A soul is incarnated on earth not only for their learning but it may come back to help other souls. When a soul chooses to leave, it may be denying another soul the opportunity to learn. Often people/souls need to learn compassion, caring for others. If a soul leaves quickly, the opportunity for the remaining souls to learn is lost. A soul always has free will. When the going gets tough, they can leave or accept the lessons that they are meant to have. Souls also have the choice to help others, remain selfish and look only after themselves or learn and help the universal needs.*

Euthanasia is a tough and delicate topic to discuss. This is also the same with suicide. Both have positive points in their favor. There are also contrary ones. This passage came at a time when both topics were being fought heavily. I have included it for your information, for your help and peace of mind if you need it at this time.

In the middle of this passage, they talk about moving on from sorrow. They certainly do not mean that we should not grieve. Grieving is one of the most important processes of the human experience. They are recommending that, as humans, we avoid the constant dwelling on the memory — a practice that is common to so many. Sorrow is one of the important lessons that we require for our evolution. Sorrow prevents us from making future mistakes.

It is a fine line of distinction between helping others and helping yourself. Ask yourself if helping is good. The first response will be the best. Some of you call it a gut reaction and that is often the best. It is true to the soul.

Helping others is often fueling a need that the other person is not recognizing. Many counselors have to answer this question regularly. Too often, we avoid the question and insist upon helping. This only creates a dependency in someone else.

Two is an important number in your future and the future of others in your world. There will be two choices as well as two opportunities. Whenever choosing something take the second. That includes obtaining two of whatever you go after. It also means that if one volcano goes off, there will be a second one soon after in the same region.

Always carry two stones with you, two crystals, two jade, two amethyst etc. Walk two of miles, kilometers, feet, etc. Do everything twice to make sure it is complete and accurate. This means a check.

February is an important month for you and your fellow beings and friends. A lot will be made aware to you and you should follow the message and information. Many of you will doubt what comes through but take heart. The information is accurate. You simply have to take it as you see fit. Some of you will take the information literally and some will interpret. Both are correct.

When you see a client the second will follow. It is the second that you should pay attention to. The meeting will contain information for you as well.

Any multiple of two will have significance to you and your writing as well as anything you do.

For some readers, two will be the correct number for them. Others may have a special personal number. We are being told that listening to our number and blending it into our lives is one of the best things we can do for ourselves.

Freedom. *Freedom means different things to different people and it is not something that should be assumed, that all want the same freedom. For many people freedom means peace, others it means no responsibility. When we want to help people, we must first ask, "What do you want?" "What does freedom mean to you?" Only then can you help and give them as much as you are capable. Everyone in the world is free. The definition simply differs.*

Playing *is so necessary to your pleasure and yet so often people on your world forget to have fun. Even* *we like to play. We will play with individuals when we see that you are getting too serious. Play keeps you from being in the small **now**. Watch your animals and see how much they play. You have a bird called a blue jay that is not too popular and yet it plays so much and mocks people who are too serious. **Play** as much as you can. Nothing is so important that you can't stop and have fun. You will always have time to get serious and do what must be done. Today you looked at the sky and saw holes in the sky. Have you ever thought about jumping from hole to hole and see how far you can jump and reach in a single walk Even pretend to stretch the edges of the holes and see what happens. You may even be able to fit other clouds into the space and blow them away! I know if you talked about this with others, they would think it strange. However, I suggest you pursue and in time they too will enjoy the hole hopping instead of complaining about your weather. Make up your own rules if you feel your game must have rules.*

Playing and having fun is so important in our life. Our souls are put on the Earth Plane to learn various lessons. There is no reason why they can't have fun. If you doubt this, think of the learning you have done, particularly at school. Which lessons are still with you today?

Energy is like a waterfall. *The more it is allowed to run free, the clearer and more abundant it will become. Flowers beside the waterfall, help to make the water more pure with more oxygen. The same with energy. The more nature that is surrounding the* *energy, the more pure and the more oxygen will be available to it. This applies to all forms of life, not just your human. Some of your city people have recognized the need for nature and put parks in the concrete city but there is still not sufficient and this is one reason for the violence that is present in your world. If people would make an effort to be surrounded more with nature, they would be less inclined to anger and violence. Even those who cannot get out into the country can provide nature by growing plants in a small garden or in a window. They can take the time to be present and practice moving the energy of their body while present in this garden or nature. This would help balance the world.* **All** *people can achieve this. Unfortunately, some people are not made aware of this need. It is the one thing that could be taught to all people without violating their culture or beliefs. Martial arts, used as they were intended, is a good medium for the young. Suggest joining forces with someone who knows the arts and develop a program that will combine both.*

When you look at the **past events in this life**, *you are dealing with details that are unimportant. A past life gives you information that you can use today to show you the strengths and lessons that you have. During this life the details are so minute that they are unimportant. Your people often use the expression, "can't see the forest for the trees". Looking at what has happened in* **this** *life is like looking at a leaf of a tree. Looking at past lives is like looking at a huge forest. It will tell you what kind of trees grow in this* *climate, what you need to plant and what major changes are needed. What do you need to harvest for use? A large forest will have some trees ready for felling to be use for furniture, etc. It also has small seedlings that are ready to grow and become something. This life gives you none of that. Even if you look at your past lives and discover what you must learn this life, you cannot change what you have done so far this life. You can only go forward. It is useless to spend time analyzing what you have learned or done that matches other lives. If you repeat a lesson, so what? You will simply have it stronger for your soul completion.*

*It is also important to let go of past life information and sorrows. They are no longer relevant. Revenge does not matter. Again, if you look at the forest as your history. If there is a tree that you don't want, removing it, or ignoring it will alter the image of the forest. Pruning it does the same. Worrying about hardships done to you in a past life is like trying to remove a tree in the forest. You are simply trying to alter a forest and making it something that was not meant to be. Look for the Eagle whenever you start to think about lessons from the past — life or present. The eagle will help you **see** what is important in this life. Remember his eyes are sharp. The spirit eagle is larger than your reality and therefore, the eyes are even larger and sharper. Good luck.*

I have intentionally kept the "Hellos," "good lucks," and other personal comments in the passages. They are reminders that our spirit guides are loving and gentle and only want what is best for us. I mentioned it before but I have kept the wording as the information came through to me. Since they don't live on our Earth, the word choice is not always the best from our point of view.

The following pages contain channeled information without any comments. They may not appear to relate to **Inner Bridges,** but all the information helps bring you into balance both within yourself and with all that is around you. For the studious reader, you may feel confused at times. You may feel that it appears out of sequence. You are probably correct. This is not meant to test you! Just remind yourself that the information came in random order. For the logical human mind, the book had to follow some order, not always the order of the universal messengers.

*Only you have the **capability to clip your wings**. You have the power to decide to fly high and free. Living with memories or in the past will clip one wing. Thinking about the future and what might happen will clip the other wing. Either way, you cannot fly. By staying in the present and choosing to fly high and free, you will stay in balance and will then be able to enjoy life as it is meant to be lived. Life is a wonderful gift that we gave you. Unfortunately so many of you do not accept the gift. When your soul entered the body at birth, there were contracts that had to be filled. In the past, the contracts are completed. Also in the future, some will be met. It is only in the present that you have the ability to make choices. These choices will affect* *what you complete and how high you will soar. **No one** can make those choices for you. Only you can decide what path is best for you. Even if you make the wrong choice in the future, you will still be in balance. You will simply be flying at a different level. No choice is wrong. This is why living in the past and worrying about what might have been is keeping you on the ground. All decisions were correct, they just have a different outcome. Enjoy life and don't clip your wings.*

A wishing well should be for things that are achievable and not for "might have been". When someone does go to a wishing well, they should go with the plans to meet the goal, or wish, that they are asking for. When we see someone has the plans, then we will give all the help we can.

Go with the flow.

And be free.

Love is an institution.

Stuck in the minds of your people that without church or family, there can be no Love. What is needed is for the institutions to break down and while there would be a struggle for a time, the individual would set their own beliefs and realize that love can go beyond the boundaries of race, country, church and family. The family would still exist but not the narrow confines of today. You are already seeing changes with divorce and many partners. Some move on and love all and others are stuck with hate and resentment of what was "done" to them.

How can this be achieved? Over many years and some turmoil, those who need structure will still have it but will be less likely to follow unquestioningly. Smaller churches, freer are coming up. Those who have egos and need to lead will be connected to these churches. Others will make their own private "church."

Fish. *Fish has many connotations your world. It is nutrition. It is leisure. It is searching It is a test of wills. For you right now the fish represents the searching but the fish has been caught. It does not represent food because you have all the fish you need. It does not represent floundering because your search has ended, for now, and you are swimming in a steady stream. You go where the stream flows and you go where the universe/spirit takes you and you accept that. You are no longer fighting to swim upstream. You will be the bait that people come to nibble on and it will be your responsibility in life from now on to feed them as much as they can eat and send them in the right direction in the stream. It also represented leisure for you because you are no longer struggling but at peace and will move gently.*

You combined the two words **peace** *and* **integrity** *during a conversation. They are the most important that any person can have. Help people understand the blend.*

When you talk about money not being important, you could let people know about the two words and they will help others reach a decision. **Peace** *and* **integrity** *cannot be achieved without each other. When you have both, money is not important. We, on the other side will help.*

When you look at people in history of your world and select the ones that you admire, you will find that they have the blend of peace and integrity. Peace comes from helping others, being true to yourself and above all having integrity in everything you say and do.

Follow your heart. *This is a belief that so few of your people practice. They may believe it but instead will look for money instead of this practice. If you took a room full of people and asked they to describe who they were. They would not state their deep belief systems nor admit that they were anything other than what was expected. For you, my child, you must follow your heart and not give in to urges to become who you are not. By this we mean that something may sound exciting and it is tempting to get some of this excitement but the peace does not come through it. Your society's way of identity and pleasure is almost always through excitement. Yes, this may mean no movies, no social clubs, no crowds and no gatherings but you will be much happier and will live longer as a result. Your book will give you peace and benefit people more than if you socialized with them. Whenever you start to feel an excitement from something coming up, ask yourself **who are you**. If the answer is other than your true self, then you are straying from following your heart.*

If you need to get money in order to meet your needs, then make the jobs as close to your heart as you can. A smoky quartz will dispel any bad energy that comes into your home.

*All the new disease that surrounds you is a result of the body not being in balance. It is also often a key or trigger to the importance of returning to center. When people are sick, they tend to spend so much time trying to heal the little parts that are sick that they forget that when their body is in balance, they will be able to reject any illness or foreign bodies. This applies to iron poisoning, and other toxins that enter the body. The person has to learn what is true to their higher self and **then** they will be able to look for physical answers. However, they must first look for the spiritual balance that is needed. People must learn to accept ideas and information that comes to them and not question or doubt. Unfortunately you are so bothered by society and other people who pretend to listen rather than listening to your own inner voice. Even when we listen to other people who talk about the importance of listening to our inner voice, you may agree but will return to what society says is best.*

Being a "stranger" *in life is only a means to finding out your truth and living with your integrity. People who challenge and reject you, are put on the planet as part of the master plan to test you. The more people you meet that reject or challenge you without you giving up, the more certain you are to keep your integrity.*

Today you asked what you needed and we told you to "paint the future." We then showed you a bald children, white hair and barren lands. This is only one part of the future. It sounds bad but it is really a good picture when you consider that the baldness puts *everyone on an equal basis There is no hair or individual beauty for people to worry about. By showing this image, you can stress the importance of people not worrying about themselves but being concerned about others as anonymous people. Everyone has a soul and that is what people must learn to see and relate to. Beauty is not important. In some of your past lives, the ones you have been seeing lately, you were looking at people in terms of their needs. For example when you were a witch and gave herbs as remedies, you did not look at or care whether they were moneyed or poor. You gave what they needed. That is where you must go today. When people need something, you must give it. Yes, it is OK to accept money for readings because the information is not **needed** but rather something to guide the person on their way. You will begin to see how money can tie you down and shift the focus of your thoughts. Today and forward, be aware of the energy around you, give information readily but encourage people to want readings so that they can start to think about their future and make some changes.*

People are gradually starting to get the message that local is better to balance the energy. For now, have people start to think local in whatever terms works for them. Many will think they are helping their local area while others will think they are helping their own health. They do not need to be so concerned about the energy except that is a justification for their actions. Starting shortly, you can start to prove the difference in energy balanced by local and energy not balanced at all. You were right when you said it has nothing to do with electrical energy. It is a much simpler form of energy. However, it is so simple that people lose sight of it as a necessary resource.

For now, draw the future.

Life is basic but humans need to be reminded so often. If there was anything that should be stored and shared are the two words: **light** *and* **balance**. *These will bring peace and happiness to all in the universe.*

You joke with your guides about the need for money and material things on Earth and they joke back. Look at life on Earth in terms of those two words, balance and light. If someone has balance or balances their material wealth, they will never feel they need more. If light is brought into a life, there will be satisfaction and peace. Light brings balance and balance brings light. No entity can live with only one. Even the spirit worlds needs these; it is just described on a different words and feelings.

Many of the changes in life we bring upon ourselves. When we stop to think about what we want in life, we never stop to think about how to get there. We are so easily swayed by the social norms and perceived **needs** *that we truly do not think about what is best for us. When the MONKS (a channeled energy) talked last night about babies and small children knowing the connection, what is best and how we bring our children up according to our rules, they were correct. Ask any small child, say 4-5, what they want and what they want to be and you will get a truer* *picture. They are also more concerned with nature and the world.*

You bring up your children in the best way possible but how bad can it be for the child. As you are aware, you do not own any child. Each child comes into the world with their own plan and desires. Many people get an astrological chart done for babies but how many get a channeling to find out what the plan is for the child and how parents can help the child. This is something that you can truly do and give a gift. You and your group have looked at the Michael roles. You are capable of getting the details and this is something that each child can benefit from.

Trees are capable of being big enough to reach into space. We also ignore the juice of the tree which is the sap. This is vital to our life force.

Has anybody looked at the eating habits of those who fight others, they let their egos interfere. If they did, they would find that people on the Earth Plane will become agitated when they don't get the best nutrition and will then pick a fight. Yes, there are other factors but most can be solved by diet. The right diet will leave the body calm and this will allow the spirit to be at rest, or at peace, within itself.

The spirit will remember the love that is available to all beings in the universe. They will realize that ego, being the one to get it right are all unimportant. We are all part of the grand total and all have the same reason for being alive. Everyone's spirit in this universe is here to exist in peace. This is why they can help other universes when they are in trouble. Yes, *there are many universes besides yours. It is your ego that leads you to think you are alone. Life exists only for the purpose of enjoying the beauty that is around us. This is one reason that the Earth was created. It was given so many beautiful, peaceful parts that it was meant to be available for all beings from any galaxy. What have you done? You have polluted your planet. You have grown the wrong foods. You have developed a way to worship a currency that is not needed. All this because a few beings discovered they could control others. This is a mistake that was made a **long** time ago. All who live today and in years to come have the ability to change this mistake. You can feed your spirit and this will feed the **Total** and then people will be able to live in love and peace. **It is possible and it is coming.** Even though each of you are a small part of the **Total,** you can make a change.*

*Taking care of your body and mind allows your spirit to rest in peace and love. This will become part of the **Total** that is available to all. Do not think this information is being given to only you. It is being given to many so that we can get beings thinking in terms of love and health. When people are healthy, they can focus their attention on peace and sharing love. We agree that there are many in your planet that do not have the food that you have but it is available. When they are shown how to get the balance according to their locale, they, too can get the love that is available. Each locale is given the right nutrients that will provide a balance for the beings who live there. We have shown you how to travel around your* *planet and stay close to a balance. Why do people not do this?*

After reading this chapter, it is a good time to go back, make notes and refer to this information as you continue reading the remainder of the book. We are given love and light from all our spirit guides and energies around us.

The Environment Connection

Honor the Wind It brings beauty, change and tranquility into our lives.

Honor the Rain. It brings nourishment, excitement and other beings

Honor the Earth. It brings food, balance and serenity.

Honor the Sun. It brings warmth, energy and peace.

How many times do we forget the balance and tranquility we receive from being out in nature? This is a give and take gift. When we receive tranquility from nature, it helps balance us internally. When a tranquil person moves through nature, the tranquility is transferred into the environment. What I see so often is that people retreat into their homes, read a few books, make a few changes in their diet or exercise program and expect to see wondrous results. It is important to understand that unlike other connections or bridges, this is the one connection that magnifies all other changes. What we absorb from the environment is magnified within our being and similarly, the state of our being is transferred into the surrounding environment. Instead of always depending upon the environment to solve your balance problems, I suggest that you give a gift to the environment by following some of the ideas and recommendations **before** you go into nature. For example, if you have read something distressing in the newspaper, take the time to balance yourself, then go for a walk in a park or near some water and consciously send loving thoughts to the Earth and other parts of the World. This **does** make a difference.

We have talked about going out in nature to get into balance and to balance nature. This may sound simple and only one way. It is not. Human beings can do much for the Earth Plane when they themselves are balanced. We also spoke about learning to alter your inner energy when you feel a change is needed. Once this has been mastered by many, then it is possible to minimize disasters on the Earth Plane.

Let us explain. Your scientists can predict earthquakes and volcanoes. Human beings who are in balance can get together as a group or at the same time and slow their own energy down. This slower energy is transferred to the Earth Plane and then slows pending disasters. Forest fires and high winds can be handled the same way. We do this on many planets. Humans are close to the stage where they can do it also. Again, use all the tools you are being taught until your vibrational level changes.

For yourself, the individual, look at what you need and turn to the environment. If you are moving at a slow energy, your society has provided easy solutions. Go to the city with the crowds and high microwave energy. Turn your electrical equipment on. Use colors red, orange, bright green and stones and aromas to match.

If you need slowing down, again turn to your environment. Trees, grass, water are the best options. Your planet is lucky to have these.

There are parts of your environment that, without human interference do vibrate faster. Wind, red sunsets, red flowers, deserts are examples. Deserts are one of the most misunderstood. If you, in your past, have lived on a planet that is all desert, you will not be affected by its energy as much as those who have not. Trees, grass and water are amongst the best to slow energy down.

Again, we want to stress that this should not be the first answer for your balance. Answers that bring health to the body and mind will be better for the spirit. This means food and meditation.

Mankind tends to focus on their internal functioning and what they put in it as the only way to stay healthy or to move beyond spiritually. Yes, you do look at pollution but only in terms of how they affect your internal functions. **Why** *do you not realize that the environment that you have created on the Earth Plane is so important that those of other lands envy you and wish that they could duplicate what is present. There are many things that can be done to improve the Earth Plane and some are doing it. You should be concerned with how you relate to the Earth Plane around you. It has a direct impact. You may recall someone suggesting that each human being should spend a day in silence and take this time to* **hear** *the sounds of the plants growing. If you tuned into the body well enough, you would hear the plants and* *animals crying. Crying because they are being ignored and cannot help themselves. When your species moves beyond the 3rd dimension into the 4th and 5th, you will hear this crying as routinely as you hear all your busy sounds that surround you today. It is not necessary to wait for this transition of your bodies and spirit. We recommend that you start working on this right now. It can be done in parallel to the foods adjustment, exercise and all other changes. You will be busy!*

*Some of you may think this is too much to complete at any one time. Not so. By taking one task out of **each** category, you can easily complete them all. We suggest that you set up a time table. (You humans do like to be organized and to plan!) It is simple. Day one, you change one thing you eat and one way that you interact with the environment. Next day, you continue these and add one more, etc.*

Again, we want to remind you that one of the focuses should be getting in balance with the region you live in so that you can then move from region or planet easily and readily without major adjustment. How is this done? Within a year of making committed changes to how you proceed with all these recommendations, your body will be ready to accept other changes. You will notice that travel, for instance, is not that difficult. Again, some of the changes made take a couple of generations but if you follow through with the changes and teach the children well, it could take less that that.

Again, we say, start small within your own lives and this will spread to your circle of friends and then beyond to towns, cities and then countries.

*At all times, think **peace** when you make these adjustments. Peace and Love makes changes so much easier to include when you make changes.*

Later, we will talk more about the dimensions and what each one will bring you. Right now, you do not need the motivation. Change will be motivation enough.

Go in peace.

Walking in mud is something that people have forgotten how to do. Yes, your climate is cold for much of the year but when the weather is warm enough, take off your shoes and walk in the mud. Feel the mud moving between your toes. When it is too cold, put boots on and walk and splash. Feel it in your fingers and feel the movement. Look at it. Study it. Even the color has a yellow tone to it. It is good for the soul.

Mud connects us with the Earth and through it, the universe. Get in touch with your surroundings and listen to what the Earth is telling you. Since mud is also very healing, you will pick up the properties through your skin to heal your very being or essence. Even though this can be a serious subject, we must remember a major part of the theme of the messages that came through the channeling — **play**. Human Beings have spent so much time working and worrying that we forget how to play. Living in balance does not always mean organized planning. It can be as simple of romping for a while and then working for a while. Play is the best way to bring our body into balance with the spirit and the mind. We may not think of play as healing but when we play we are not asking the mind to perform any function, thereby allowing it to connect with our spirit and heal the body. All animals and birds play. Why shouldn't we?

We have taken a light hearted look at playing in the mud but it is time to go back to the serious side. Connecting with the Earth has a significant effect on the soul's intent as well as the well-being of the Earth and Universe. Many people go into meditation, or centering, to heal the body and connect with their higher self. Consequently, they forget the importance of healing the Earth and connecting with the nature spirits. These spirits have as much love and information as the spirit guides from the Universe and should not be ignored. Some believe that all spirit energy must live some of their lives as nature spirits as well as entering the physical plane.

We, as physical creatures have the responsibility of bridging the energies in the two worlds, Earth and Universe. When we center ourselves through meditation, and prayer, we need to ask for healing for all, energy for all and love for all. When even a small part of the population does this, they can counterbalance the damage that is done by others in the physical world. When this energy dart grows in size, it is enough to start a change in the other physical energies.

The passage about mud is a simple way to remind us that connection can be made in many ways and we do not have to depend on centering alone. Play is healing!

Gardens: *If you have a garden around your home, it is important that you plant it to compliment and blend with the environment around it. For example, in a rainforest, plant rainforest plants. It is also important that should you want to have agitating colors, such as a red rose, that you have more of calm around to make it balanced. A rose garden is not calming and serene because the flowers are more active. They should be placed in a garden that will balance it and keep it calm.*

When they talked about roses not being calm, they are referring to the thorns. Thorns are for protection. This can be inferred as fighting the environment around the rose. Therefore, we want to calm this fight. When the rose is a soft or peaceful color this helps balance the survival instinct of the bush.

There is no reason why we can't have exotic plants in our garden but we must remember to include plants that are original and indigenous to the region where we live . The one aspect of a faster and changing lifestyle is that we have learned to want what is not common around us and society is responding by giving it to us through hybridization and importing. Consequently, we must take responsibility for our own lives and desires.

If you choose to have tropical plants such as orchids in your home, make sure that they are surrounded with plants that are calm. Again center an orchid in a display of green plants. Look at the colors that are in the flowers and make sure they are calm or are balanced.

If tropical plants such as orchids come from a greenhouse in your area, they will be closer to the region's vibration. Ask how many generations of plants have been grown locally. You may find that you get strange looks, but this information is important. One of the benefits of many tropical plants is the colors. Again, when you choose the plants, look at the colors and what they will do for you.

All areas need the benefit of meditation to help bring us up to a 4D vibration.

Meditation has been credited with the ability to still the mind and to purify the body from toxins and negative thoughts. If we do have these toxins and thoughts, they get carried beyond our body into the environment. Therefore, the purification must spread beyond our bodies to the area around us. The best way that we can help the environment and our planet is by meditating outside as much as possible. This also helps all creatures that exist in our garden or region of the planet.

The use of local art and supplies will play havoc with the economy of the world. However, when we become a global community, this will not be an issue since we will all have similar items from our local region. It is possible to create all luxuries and tools that we use from any region in the world. The mix will just be different. When you live in a desert, you will use a different stone than if you live in a rainforest. Both make pots and tools.

All physical belongings that we have in our homes carry the energies of the raw products as well as the energies of those who made them. When you surround yourself with items from afar, it is more difficult to bring your body into balance. Should you doubt this, consider your reaction when you go into a home that contains furniture from other regions such as rattan or mahogany. What is their art like? How do you feel? Now consider how you feel when you are in a building with local art and furniture such as pine. Do you feel totally relaxed?

Surround yourself with rocks from your region. The energy is very different. The ions and carbon [carbon dating] *in rocks is absorbed through your skin and lungs. When it is not from your region, it becomes a foreign substance that your body has to fight. It jars the energy and the body becomes confused. If you have one or two foreign objects in your home, make sure there is a **big** piece of rock or sculpture in the house that you can go past frequently* [local]. *This helps balance the energy entering your body.*

When you become tuned into the energy of items surrounding, you will be able to pick up a stone or gem, take a few moments and tell the emotions or story of that rock. This shows you how the energy of items can vary. Every time you expose yourself to foreign energy, you need a counter balance to bring your body back into equilibrium.

Another possibility is to take local rocks, place them in water (spring, pure and local) (or surround the water with rocks). Place your hands near the container so that you can pick up the energy. Meditate for a few minutes, breathing in the local air. The remedies of gems and rocks are not always useful unless they are balanced with local rocks. The exception to this is crystals. These come from the heart of the earth and contain all DNA and energy of the entire world. Should you travel to another region, it is good to take a piece of crystal with you. It should have lived in your region for some time, the larger part of your life, the better. This will help you align your energy with the foreign region.

The first part of this channeled information is an alternative way to surround yourself with local energy. This process is similar to gem essences. You have a choice. You can absorb the energy through your hands. Or, if you prefer, you can swallow the energy by placing a few drops of the essence under your tongue.

Every home should include at least **one** crystal, the larger the better. It is important to remember that unless you are balanced, a large crystal may throw you out of balance. A crystal easily absorbs energy from everything around it.

Carry a piece of crystal with you when you go into places that have plants or objects that will through your energy out of balance. At this time, it is very *important to consume foods that are **Best** for you. Otherwise, you will become so out of balance that it will take longer to balance and you are subject to more absorption through the skin.*

At the beginning of this section, they talk about introducing one change at a time. However, as you progress in your changes, or crossing the bridges, you will understand that all the information and the methods are intended to be blended and combined. This passage is one example of using the foods and the environment adjustments in combination to balance your body and the environment.

*Gradually get rid of art objects in your home that are not from your region. If you cannot get rid of them, place **all** objects in a single location, behind glass. This will minimize the leakage of the energy. Make sure that they are behind glass, not artificial glass [Plexiglas]. The room can also be balanced with plants that are local and lots of green. Green energy is slow and will help to bring the energy of the objects into a balance with yours.*

The plants should be adjacent to the foreign art objects. It is also best not to have the art of a different region near your favorite chair.

Items from different regions, art and foods, are the main reason that the population is so ill and there are so many strange illnesses!

Becoming ill from eating while you travel is a common complaint. Most talk about the 24-hour flu or Montezuma's revenge. We humans tend to ignore the illnesses that we bring home with us. Indigenous people adapt to bugs, pollution, foods from their locale. Even with the world becoming smaller with international travel, we forget that our immune system cannot adapt quickly. Take it slow and when ever possible, carry foods from your region for a few days when you travel long distances.

Mountains were created through an imbalance in nature and your world. There are small living beings in all objects. They were the ones that went out of balance to create the mountains. Over time, they learned to balance their energy, but many years ago, they did not know how. The same thing is happening to humans today. Unless the population learns to balance themselves with nature and the universe, the same thing will happen, mountains of a different sort. The pressure is building up and it is important that you learn to get in balance with what that is around you. Going into the mountains and forest areas will teach you how to get that; if you are willing to take the time to listen.

Many people in our world do not think there is anything they can do to stop natural disasters such as volcanoes. This is not so. When we connect with the Earth Plane, meditate and balance everything around us, disasters can stop. It is most important to take the time to listen to the Earth and all its creatures.

Smoke can be a very calming and balancing if we look at it the right way. When we see clear white smoke coming out of something, we feel calm. When it is black and blowing, it causes the agitation in us. We see the wind and our internal energies moving at a different rate. White smoke is slow and clear.

Smoke can just be another type of cloud. We pick up the energy of the color and the motion. Red smoke (fire) is similar to our root chakra and can indicate that our survival is at risk. Blue smoke is calm, as is white. Both are pure. Pollution smoke is brownish-gray. When our instinct and intellect is blocked, our chakra colors become very muddy. This is exactly what pollution does to the population. It dulls the oxygen intake and this slows the brain. Smoke, therefore, is a good indicator of what is happening to both us and the Earth Plane. The entities commented on black clouds and blowing wind causing agitation. It is the wind that caused the agitation. The black usually indicates rain, which is cleansing.

When people talk about the danger of earthquakes and how they had better be ready, they are missing the whole point. Physical preparation is not what is important. While it should not be ignored, it is more important to plan for a place to meditate and how to maintain your spiritual balance in your life. Being worried and panicky over the physical needs of the body and family will only throw the body out of balance. By body, we are talking about the 3 levels, physical mental and spiritual. Keeping the spiritual in balance will automatically help to bring the other two into balance.

When a earthquake kit is prepared, people tend to ignore the balance of foods and how important it is to make sure that all goods come from the region where *you live. When care packages are sent to other regions, people will send foods that **they** want, ignoring what the best foods are for those who receive it. Canned goods, **may** be O.K. but it important to sort out the packages according to the region they are going to. Often the care packages are made up with the giver's needs in mind. People in the tropics will not know how to use foods of the forest region. Same as forest disaster areas may not know how to use corn meal of the desert. It will take a great deal of managing to supply the people of the earth with the best foods. Again, those who have been working on bringing their bodies into balance will be best prepared for any disaster. Should they have to eat foods that are not best for them, their **pure** body will be better able to get back into balance. When people are panicking over the physical disaster such as flood or earthquakes, they get caught up in the mania of the crowd and forget to honor their own spiritual being.*

I received a stone from some ancient ruins recently. Both the person who found it and myself were amazed at how much agitation and terror we were able to sense when we held this stone. History tells us that the people in this area ran in panic and terror when a cataclysmic event occurred. Could this have been an earthquake? If the people were panicky, this agitation was transferred to surrounding environment. They probably would not have understood this but we are different. For us, plans for our physical survival should be extended to include several possible locations where we could stop for a brief meditation.

Since it is highly unlikely that people will be willing to take the time and money to sort food out according to regions, an alternative could be to have local water ready to help balance the body. Purification tablets will allow residents of a region to drink their own water. This, then minimizes the imbalance in the individual. Therefore, they have a better chance of survival.

Honor the Wind. It brings beauty, change and tranquility into our lives.

Honor the Rain. It brings nourishment, excitement and other beings.

Honor the Earth. It brings food, balance and serenity.

Honor the Sun. It brings warmth, energy and peace.

We need to always remember that all aspects of the environment will bring peace to us.

Birds represent the element Air; fish, Water. Whenever we need more of one element than another, it is important that we bring the animal into our life that represents the element. Pets are not the best choice for the element. It is better to be in nature and respond to the animal that you need. When you want to know what each animal represents, it is better to ask yourself how you feel when you see that animal. It may not always agree with books.

If you do have fish at home to bring the water element, they should be fish from around your region.

Tropical fish in a northern or forest home, will upset the overall energy of those around them. It becomes more difficult to balance your inner energy when there are "foreign" fish in the house.

There are many indications when we need a particular element. Our mental and emotional states are often the easiest ways to measure the degree of imbalance. When you find you have too much of one elemental characteristic, then look to the others to bring you back into balance. For example, if you are "flighty" (air) and can't concentrate, then you need to raise your earth element. Here is what to do if you display any of these:

Air: scattered thoughts, fast and often disconnected speech, worry, sleeplessness. *To balance Air:* Fasting, soft exercise, massage, staying up later at night, cooked food

Earth: daydreaming, sluggish movements, over-planning, depression. *To balance Earth:* Rigorous exercise, staying awake, less starchy foods, more fruits.

Water: Fear, suspicion, stingy, excessive stubbornness, cold. *To balance Water:* Pungent and spicy foods, warmth, steady exercise, regular meals, minimal sleep.

These are steps that you can take without paying attention to the animal kingdom. In addition to these remedies, it is wise to go into nature and focus on the animals representing the specific element.

Lights, electricity and motor cars. *These are all inventions that make your life easier. You are given*

the ability to create so that you can make your life easier. **However,** *it is not meant to be a demanded standard. Lights should be used in moderation. Electricity is what has created your* **El Nino.** *It has warmed the water through the runoff and flowed down to warmer areas. With the water being generally warmer, it affects the entire earth. This* **El Nino** *is creating changes in your world. You are talking about it, joking about it but not taking the warning seriously. Everything is too electric. You become demanding and selfish if you can't have the best. The same is true with cars. They are designed to allow you to get around easier, but you have become so dependent on them that you have forgotten how to walk. You don't take the time to walk, enjoy the nature, friends, and community. The car has isolated you from others. There has become less support for your neighbors because you are in a car, not wanting to stop and help. This has evolved into violence. At this time of year, people give to charity and people in need and feel very* **good** *about themselves.* **But** *what about the rest of the year? You tend to ignore others. Cars allow you to go past others, not bothering to stop and help. You don't take the time to take people without a car to nature walks, and allow them to get into balance again. If you have a car and share the nature with them, more of you will come into balance and may be able to help balance the environment around. As people start to feel good about themselves, they will become more open to wanting to balance the nature and then the* *universe. They won't understand what you are talking about until they are balanced within themselves.*

I am sure many who read this will dismiss it as a reminder that is unnecessary. This is not so. Humans are **very** blasé and demanding. Look at your life, how much you interact with people. Write a small reminder to yourself and put it on your mirror. ***Today, I will do three things to help others, give love and be in harmony with the world around me.*** Make the number your choice and increase it regularly. Watch and record the changes around you.

*Music should be an integral part of your life. When you listen to music, stop and find out how you feel. If you feel energized to the point of being wound up, then it is not the best for your bodily systems. Calm music has a way of balancing the energy. When music is played loud, it can disturb the energy of nature. Music is written by the higher DNA strands. Those who compose music are already evolved. This also goes for other arts, **providing**, it is a slower pace. When a painting is vibrant, it has the effect of speeding up the energy. You should be very careful of this. If you are in a high vibrational climate, you may require specific foods to slow your energy. If the climate is a slower vibration, you may need to speed your personal energy up to match the surrounding nature. However, once you are in tune, then you should remove the paintings and replace with softer paintings. The same goes for music. Even if you find music that will balance your energy, most of your day should be surrounded by silence. This way you can hear the* *sounds around you, and hear what nature is telling you. Nature tells you a lot when you stop and listen. Your insides will also tell you a lot as well. This you cannot hear if you are busy listening to music, noise or talking to yourself. Each person should make the time to listen to yourself. This can be achieved by meditating or starting our meditating and then moving into nature. Each leaf has a sound. Each bird has a sound. Each insect has a sound. It is important that we all become aware of each sound. For when the time comes that we need to rescue the small ones, we will know the sounds and be able to make sure that we have all the best, the most healthy.*

It is well known that music, color and vibration in general is speeding up your personal vibration. We accept that as a 'fact of life' and do not feel that anything can be done to change this. This is not so. When we, as individuals, decide **not** to purchase loud music or paintings, then the artists will begin to understand.

Consider the time when music became loud, vibrant and often discordant. In the 1950s and '60s, people were starting to recognize that war was not the best way to solve world problems. I believe that this is when higher powers stepped in and introduced us to the loud music. To them, it seemed to be the only way that they could control the forces on this Earth Plane. Therefore, they planted ideas in our minds. Look back in history and when there was a composer or artist that produced vibrant art, check what was going on in their country. For now, we can become selective and use this music and art to balance our energy and then switch over to pleasures that will bring harmony to our bodies.

Energy is like music. The universe and the world is moving at a set rhythm. If you are vibrating at 1/4 time or triple time, it is OK as long as your beat is hitting at the beginning or end of the earth's time. Disharmony or imbalance will occur when those beats are not set at the exact time. Another example would be moving down a river or ocean. If you move at the exact speed at the current, no problem. However, if you move at a slower or faster speed that is synchronized there is no problem. However, this is difficult.

When furniture or art is man-made it is in perfect harmony with your earth region and your body. If it is completely manufactured by machines, then it is imbalanced to your region. It is important for your well being to surround yourself with as much natural and man-made as possible. It is important that you go up into the mountains or hills and spend some time, each day is fine. This will give you extra information. For each person, there is hills in all regions, stay with the climate where you are living. If you move around, then take a few days at the normal height before traveling up to the mountains. The imbalance is greater and is more difficult for the body to balance. Each person should learn how to feel energy so that they know what is going to be good. By feeling the energy around, this sends a message to the body and the body, if in good balance, will be able to adjust more quickly.

All things on this Earth carry energy. It is important that we remember this when we are working on building or creating something. Should we be in an angry mood, this is transferred to our creation. Others pick this up. Fortunately, it won't be long before we return to the time when furniture and other items are carrying the love of the artist. It is so simple to share love with others by creating in a simple, calm and peaceful manner.

They talk about traveling up mountains. The energy of each mountain differs, as does the region. Therefore, honor your body and allow it to balance to the region before forcing another change, such as height.

*Hummingbirds are a very peaceful bird and since all regions have them, they should be encouraged to come to feeders. The feeder should be filled with pure water and sugar with **no** chemicals added. Or a fruit juice will be the best. When you have hummingbirds in your area, other birds and wildlife will follow. Spend some time regularly outside **talking** to the wildlife. You will find that they will start coming to you when you start to talk to them. They will come for company, not just when they have a message. People in your world have to become aware that **all** wildlife have a message for you and they should listen and pay attention. Even when an animal stays away, it is giving you a message. It is usually telling you that you are doing things right and no further information is necessary. If* *they stay away for a while and then return, it is usually telling you that you didn't get the message the first time and they are giving you a second, or third chance! Take it.*

Many books have been written about the messages of animals. Unfortunately, most ignore the messages until they are desperate for an answer to a dilemma. They forget to look for messages in the good times! Usually people agree with the writings but often we will have our own personal information. When this happens, follow your own interpretation and not the information from someone else.

Fir trees, fir essence, pine *are all good for moving toward the balance and ultimate.*

Hawk, Eagle and Raven. *They are all powerful and mystical birds. Yet, are they any more mystical than any of the other birds? Why do you revere these birds and not the crow or sparrow? In a dry climates, is the roadrunner respected? Many of these birds that are in your world are not respected as are birds that have learned to adapt to your society. The first three are maintaining their own world. Birds and animals that have adapted have become less respected, hunted and therefore become extinct. Bears have gone from looking for food naturally and instead they looked at garbage dumps (which would not be there if you have lived as you should). Bears start to be hunted by your beings because they can no longer find food on their own. They have become dependent. This is happening to you as well. You have become dependent on other people giving you what you need. It is not the best for* *you. In order to become respected and revered, you should start to look back at your origins and decide that is best for you. Is garbage, chemicals best for you. No. The best for you is natural, pure food that is according to your region. You do not to eat oranges in the north. The dry climates do not need to eat lush food. All of you can eat according to your origin, just like the birds and animals. When this gets lost, creatures get lost and start acting for selfish, frightened reasons. This is happening to you now. It is time and important that you return to your origins. You should eat what is natural for your region, to balance the energy and eat as pure as you can. All small plots of land are best for growing what you need. A human does not need a large piece of land to grow his food. Evolution has given you conveniences that you can use to preserve the foods. A little work is not a bad idea either. The three birds we talk about are still looking for their natural food. It is when you won't let them live where they have always lived and have polluted their food that the trouble arises. Continue to respect them but also respect the other creatures that you are destroying. All creatures are honored by other creatures and will be protected before the humans who do not understand.*

This passage is giving us an important message and reminds us that we cannot live without nature and the environment. We must learn to honor the complete planet and all who live on it. Each contributes. Studying the Eagle, Hawk and Raven in nature we can notice how they are almost meditating and listening to what is being spoken. Animals who try to adapt to our invasion, lose sight of the signs from the environment. This is causing them many problems.

Look at your sky and what do you see. Do you see dark clouds and cast a depressing shadow?. Do you see bright portions. Do you see random patterns that provide opportunities for creation and fun. Do you look at the reflection in the water; enjoying but afraid to look at the real thing. The sky is a reflection of each persons life. To each person it appears different and how they look at it from day to day reflects their outlook on life. Each sky offers beauty and tranquility. We have only to look at it from the right angle. Reflections are never the real thing and so we will get the picture backwards and missing some of the fine details. When we see a cloud, stop and look at the beauty, dancing figures and wonder what story it will tell. Just as the clouds change from moment to moment, our life changes from moment to moment. Each second we may be happy or sad, healthy or unhealthy, troubled at peace. It is up to us to decide how we want to see our world and our life.

Often the phrase "... has his head in the clouds" is used to describe a person who is avoiding reality. This may well be so. It can also be messages for us as to how we should address a problem or issue. This is one of the safest, surest ways to back into harmony with nature. What is wrong with that?

The passage refers to the reflection in the water and being afraid see the **real** thing. We need to ask ourselves, is this the major focus of life or is it simply a way to relax and enjoy? All too often, we ignore gifts that are given to us and spend our time rushing around. Stop and see the patterns and smell the roses. We need this time be ourselves.

Clouds. *There are layers of clouds that you see when you look up at the sky. Each layer represents past and future lives of our souls. The more dense and the more of them often indicates the number that you are dealing with in your present life. People choose to live in a region where there are clouds that will help them clear up past issues of their souls. When you look at the clouds, mark or spot specific areas. These are meant for your learning at that time. You will often see dark clouds that seem to form a tunnel through to lighter clouds above. This tunnel is telling you that you should take the risk and go through the tunnel to a higher cloud. The lessons to be learned at that time are there waiting for you. When you see a hole or window, it is telling you that a spirit has just gone through. This is how the souls leave your plain and travel beyond. Sometimes you know who and sometimes not. It is quite appropriate to wish them farewell and ask that you see them later.*

Jagged edges of the clouds usually will tell you that there are lessons to be learned. Do not be afraid. You are always given the strength to handle those edges and you will never be hurt or cut by them. A way to identify the lessons is simply to sit and concentrate on the cloud and the edge and ask in a meditation what lessons it has for you. Unfortunately, there is little time taken in your lives to learn what is waiting for you. Take the time. Nature and your world has so much to teach. We on the other side, try very hard to find ways to give you information and ways that you can learn. Clouds will give you a tunnel to a specific life, edges to learn from, wispy gauzy clouds that you can look through, silver linings, rainbows, they are all there for you to enjoy and learn from. When you ask why spirits or souls settle in different parts, they are there to learn lessons that that region will teach them. Again, learning to live and eat from that region will speed up their learning.

You are learning from being in the garden and in your walks. It is a shame that more people do not do this. We try to be creative. By being creative in opening your eyes and mind, you can be creative and joyful as well

Continue to look at the sky with the new information. Also look at how pure it is. What can you do to make it purer and what can you do to help others see the pureness in life. Even dryer regions have the clouds that they can look at to reflect their own life. By looking at the clouds, you are seeing an image of your life but it is NOT a mirror image. It is a way to see yourselves with symbols. This is not mirror. This is the real thing!

Much is written about clouds, the formations and the colors. It is also a reminder to us to stop and pause in our busy lives to look at these beautiful presents from nature.

Clouds are like bouncing balls. Everyone needs to have a lighthearted playtime. Can you imagine bouncing big beach balls as you walk under the light clouds above?

The trees and plants that you respond to will also indicate who you are in your life and the work you need to do. Willows will show you how flexible you are. Trees with a lot of leaves and evergreens usually show that you want to hide your feelings from others, often even from yourself. If you hide your feelings in a tree, look at how you can fly beyond the tree and share your feelings and wisdom. There is much that can be used by others, they just have to realize that this knowledge is also for them. In time they will learn.

So many people do not think their emotions or ideas are important. Many assume that everyone has the same experience. Even if this is so, how we respond to each experience is not the same. Our responses are made according to our life plan. Sharing our responses will be recorded in the collective unconscious and therefore speed up the learning process of those on this Earth Plane.

The ozone layer is diminishing as you know. Most of you are worrying about skin cancer but you don't talk about other effects on your planet. One of the effects is the bleaching of all your beautiful colors in flowers. Your world is blessed with so many colors that you do not realize the other worlds are gray. If the abuse continues, you will see the world becoming more like other worlds, like your outer homes.

When we live in a region that is bleached, we are not aware of this gradual change. Making a continuous trip through ozone affected areas and one that is not will draw this to your attention. The scientists are already discovering that the coral and other life is become affected by changes in nature. It is within our capabilities to slow this change.

When making furniture and equipment from twigs, it is important to remember to ask permission. Even though a piece of wood is old and looks dead, it is very much alive. There are energies that need to give permission. When it is left in its natural state, it is providing a home and purpose to nature. When you remove it from there, the wood and creatures inside need understand the higher purpose and good. All too often your people will remove wood and make things that are not for the need for survival but for luxury, such a waste!

When we meditate regularly and become familiar with our physical responses, we will be able to **hear** the answer when we ask permission. This can be done through several methods. One is to silently ask and **listen** to your inner voice. Another is to place your hand on the wood and **feel** the answer. This is not difficult but it requires listening to our body. Yoga, Meditation, TM™ and other relaxing techniques will help you to become aware of the messages you receive.

Each person has a specific gem or rock that resonates at the same frequency. This has nothing to do with month or region. For example, your stone may be an amethyst. An emerald may also good for you. The best way to use these gems is to wear them with a clear crystal on each side. This will align your energy and help to keep it balanced. When you travel to different regions of the world, this stone will keep you connected to the earth.

Another way is to take two drops of the gem essence each morning. Take a small piece of the stone and crystal and put them in pure water and set them in the sun in the region where you live. After several hours prepare and store. A new blend should be made each year. This is a way of ensuring that the universal energy vibration is met.

When you go out into nature, try wearing your stones and see if you get a different reaction from the wild ones.

If people of your world want to learn what stone they should get, have them go to a rock shop and feel each stone. Then they must hold the stone for at least one minute and learn what your body is saying. They then take the stone home and live with it before making the essence. This essence is not something that someone else can do for you. It is very personal.

There are several important points in this passage. First, some stones are toxic and should be placed **around** the pure water to transfer the energy. Second, it does not have to be a precious gem. Third, it has nothing to do with your birth date. Last, the gem essence must be made by the person who will be using it. An Essence practitioner may assist but cannot make the essence for you.

While gem essences must be made by the person who will use it, flower essences should be made by someone trained and qualified in energy medicine. It is also important to use flower essences from the area you are living. Flowers will pick up the energy of the Mother Earth much faster than gems and therefore affect you much faster. Many health practitioners use many different brands of essences from around the world. They are looking for the emotional remedy that will help their client. Since we are interested mainly in balancing, we want to stay true to our locale. The emotional remedies will help to bring us back into the center but we should be more interested in the energy carried by each essence. Again, we need to remember that the color of the flower used affects the energy it carries from the Earth. This is reviewed in more detail in other sections.

There is also a disease that is being born right now in N.A. that will become deadly. It will be free of killing by all your chemicals and will spread rapidly once it is born. It will mostly affect women of middle age but will be taken by men of all ages.

Only time will tell what this disease is and how quickly we get it under control.

When you go on your shamanic journeys, you always forget the flowers and trees. They are just as important, often more important than the other spirits you call in. Remember them. Ask who they are and also ask what they help you with.

A shamanic journey is a native meditation usually with a specific purpose. Spirits and guides can be called in to help us in any meditative session. We must remember the flowers and trees whenever we meditate.

Wind is the voice of all on the other plane. When it is very windy, they are telling you that people are not listening. Take time on windy days to stop to listen. Observe the animals. What plants catch your attention? What colors? Often this will be what is needed both by yourself and others around you. People who live in a rainy climate and complain are most often those who choose not to help themselves and help to bring about change. For **all,** *change can be good or bad and life can be changed into whatever you want.*

Winds of change. *You must be ready to move with the changing wind. When the wind is stronger towards you, change and go with the flow. There is much going on in your world right now that encourages you to go with the wind of change. If the world sent healing to troubled people and they learned to change direction, then the powers (political) would have no strength and the wind would die out. The more people try to fight and go against the wind, the stronger the wind will become. At the spring equinox, encourage all to meditate and send energy over to those involved. However, it will be after the 13th when it may be too late. You yourself can do much right now.*

Each region does have a prevailing wind but when the wind changes direction, stop and look for what it is telling you. Change the direction you are moving and send out healing thoughts to all who need it. At the time this was channeled, the full moon was on the 11th. The power and strength of full moon will last for approximately two days after. When the moon is on the wane, its influence becomes weaker. We were being asked to combine the power of the wind with the power of the full moon. This will apply at any time when the moon is full.

Wind. *Wind is one of the most beneficial elements on your planet. Wind is what clears the air, clears your lungs, carries seeds to promote new growth and most of all will take you home. Your people are worried about rockets to other planets but all they need to do is learn how to read the wind and then ride it. In February, the currents are the strongest to take you to outer space as you call it. Once you are there, you can set the direction and you will get to your planet. You already know how to float or astral travel. The principle of the wind and a space ship is the same. By thinking of the destination and going with the wind, you can reach anywhere you want. You ask how this will help the average person. If they can change their thinking to view the wind as a friend. When they realize that wind will plant new seeds, feed the wild life, clean your lungs and carry allergies and infections away, they will appreciate a good windy day. The problem is that so many people consider the wind as a nuisance and think it draws the ailments to you. This is not so. The only reason it draws the ailments is because people do not keep their thoughts clear and happy, full of love. As an experiment, get a group of people together and have them all think good* *thoughts, ask for a wind to come and see if you feel good about the wind. Your native people had rain and sun dances. If you look, you will also find a wind dance among some of the nations. They all know how to call up the elements as they needed them. Your people can also. Your people are so used to having everything done for them that they forget that they are responsible for their own lives and future.*

How we think about or view what we consider as barriers to life reflects the impact the barrier becomes. So often a barrier is a great opportunity and gift.

Weeds become trees. If we left the weeds alone, they would grow and become trees. But you who live on earth like to destroy anything that does not conform to your idea of what is right, pretty and good. Weeds provide many good things. They are also living creatures. Even underprivileged people or cultures that do not conform are given foods that are less than ideal. If only people would honor all living things, the world would become filled with trees, and beauty. Weeds, like other different creatures can contribute so much but most of it is unrecognized by the average person.

A challenge for individuals who are interested. Try for one month, not to kill or judge anything they see. Instead admire the positive aspects of it whether it is a weed or ugly or handicapped person. [At the time of the channeling, I was seeing a beautiful pink with hints of purple, all glowing with a white or silver hue.]

Have you noticed when people are asked to contribute to CARE packages, they quickly and willing contribute, but only what they themselves will not eat or wear. Everyone has pride but we tend to forget this inward pride until we are struck with similar circumstances.

You asked last night about the prophecies that you have had, volcano and avalanches. Pay attention to when you get them, the dates of events around the world and you will get your answer. There are so many of us who are sending messages to friends on your planets that some may get crossed. You may pick up other messages. By paying attention, you can fine-tune your information and discover how accurate they are and over what period of time.

As we move through the 21st century, there will be an increasingly number of messages coming from our friends. We need to learn to listen for them.

[My rock on the beach became important.] *Remember that all rocks are living things. You can see the energy around it. All of nature on your planet is to be loved and cared for. By encouraging even one person to change this outlook will help to bring peace to the world. The pollution is becoming worse and the chemicals more widespread. You have survived for millions of years and most of it without any chemicals at all. Yes, you did have chemicals in the early years but you have moved beyond. Love and positive thoughts are really all that is necessary to produce what you desire. Teaching people to warm their bodies from within will reduce the need for fuel that is becoming scarce on your world. You will meet someone who is able to raise their body temperature* *through energy, meditation and thinking. This should be told to all you can. You have a lot of people living in colder areas and this will speed up the need for sharing this information. Your ever faithful wind can be used to warm up areas and homes when you do not have the ability or time to warm yourselves up. For example, as you gradually learn to achieve this feat, you will not be able to sustain the warmth **and** concentrate on other work **and** sleep. Completing all this at once is too much for a novice. This will come gradually. However, as the world moves into new eras, the people will be able to achieve this more readily.*

For now, the simplest way is to go into a meditative state, breath deep and bring a warm bubble around you. Imagine this bubble getting warmer. Feel the energy within your body heating up and moving into your toes and hands. This is similar to how people can warm themselves and their homes. Your children come onto earth with this ability but hospitals take this away by smothering with blankets. If you can ask older people in ancient civilizations how they cared for their babies, you will find out that they did not smother in blankets. The warmth of the air around was more important. This was done through body contact and sharing the heat. All children can do this and so can your adults. They just have to relearn. A rock can heat up when you concentrate on it. You are aware of a crystal warming up when you hold it and this is a good way to practice. Next move to a 'cold' stone and warm it up. Tai Chi and Gi Gong are good techniques to begin this training.

Softness of the wind
Gentle and strength as the sky
See the colors and bring them into your life.
There were bridges connecting all the planets in the sky.

We are reminded to appreciate the wind and the softness. The colors are the colors of all nationalities. They are part of us and we are one. This is the reason for the bridges connecting the planets. These bridges also connect all nations on Earth. We are one.

The ocean is filled with pollution and chemicals. The Mayan and Witaha gave you something that you fed into a funnel to provide healing for the ocean. There is no sense trying to clean up Europe and the Atlantic they are too far gone. The only place you can save is the Pacific. This is why the Maya and Witaha have left this planet because you [Earth beings] *weren't learning fast enough.*

The Mayan were on Earth in what is now Central America from approximately 1200 BC to 1500 AD. The Witaha are an ancient culture from an island off New Zealand.

You cannot get rid of chemicals and pollution without healing the peace at the same time.

Realized that VATA is Air, Ether, PITTA is Fire and Earth, KAPHA is Earth and Water. If people want to talk to angels and prepare for the universe, they need to keep their VATA at a fine balance. This is probably one reason why more people are VATA in this world. They need to look carefully at the other balance so they will recognize peace and love for everything.

VATA, PITTA and KAPHA are constitution types from Ayurveda, a life science from India. However, all parts of the world need to understand the basics of this so they can balance their internal bodies and facilitate connection with the universe.

Palms, Cactus, Cedar and Pine trees were what came though. This represents all climates. **However,** *they do not represent all regions of the world. Cedar on the West Coast does not have the same energy as a Cedar in Europe.*

This morning you saw a large Eagle that was illusory. It was real but it was the spirit of an eagle. The head was clear so that you could be sure of what bird was present. It was shown to you to remind you that the power of the Eagle is always with you. The size is to remind you that the eagle looks over many creatures and is not there for you alone. You can call on the eagle power whenever you choose. It is gentle, knowing and powerful. If you have any doubts about what is going on in life, calling the Eagle will remind you, or tell you, that things are OK.

Trouble. *Many people are in trouble or about to face trouble but do not realize it. When the clouds flow in one direction, that is good. When it is the opposite, they should be warned and learn to be cautious. From the West is a sign. East is the best for all people. When it is combined with heat, or hot winds they should be* *very careful to consume the right foods and the right amount of fluids.*

*The **tides are ebbing**. This may sound strange to some but you must realize that an ebbing tide will leave food and minerals. People are not paying enough attention to the resources around them. They are always looking beyond for bigger and better things. This is one reason for the disaster in Honduras right now. Unfortunately, people must suffer but it is showing people that there is so much that they can remove and send to others that they will stop and pause and thank. The piles of clothes shows that people do not need. If there was one message we could give your people is.*

Eat local, live simple and give thanks.

*This encompasses all a person will need. By giving thanks for what you already have, or what is given you, you will realize that it is such a small word but means so much to others. Tulips open up and smile when they receive a little sunshine and show their thanks. Other flowers and plants also do it but tulips seem to show more. Surrounding yourself with tulips and pictures is one way of reminding yourself that saying thanks is a simple thing. Each house should have pictures of the flowers in many colors. You should be able to switch the picture around according to your mood. Pictures can be a gift. Paint many and give to many. It is a simple gift. By adding small words to the gift, **some** will realize that it applies to them.*

Why always ask for the exotic when a message can be given with everyday things. The crows will give you just as much information as an exotic eagle or hawk. You do not need these fancy birds all the time.

Throughout this section, we have talked about using nature to balance yourself. We also spoke of giving to nature in return. Nature is not an unlimited resource for our use. There has already been much polluting and destruction. I encourage all readers to take time to honor their inner being before walking in your environment. This is only a small way of returning a gift that we take for granted. We also spoke of meditating in nature. Since meditation is an immediately healing, when it is done **in** nature, both worlds, our inner being and the environment receive an immediate benefit.

Meditation and Living in Balance

It is very difficult to live in balance without knowing the art of meditation. Meditation centers the mind and spirit and also heals the body. However, as we learned, it is not always the direct path to total connectedness. Much of the channeled information dealt with meditation and balance. Because there was so much material, I took literary license and have only included portions and, hopefully, did not duplicate the concepts.

Meditation. *Meditation can be done in a variety of ways. Each has its benefits and all benefit the body. It is a way of aligning the body to the universe and nature around it. It is recommended that at least an hour/day, preferably in the morning.*

We talk of meditation but it may be more appropriate to use the term **centering**. Centering because healing and balancing comes from centering the energy within your body so that it can be healed. Also centering will connect you to your higher self. Meditation is an accepted word on the Earth Plane and this is why we started using this word. However, meditation is connected with religion and the 'right' way of doing things. Centering moves all the energy either from the left or right into the center of your body. This has nothing to do with religion. Centering is part of the universal way of communication and travel. If a body is not aligned, it cannot communicate nor can it travel.

For the humans who are connected with religion and feel more comfortable talking in those terms, let us look at the Earth meditation and how it applies to the universe.

When a person meditates and uses an objective of bypassing the body and connecting to the higher self, this can be achieved without the body being in complete alignment. When a human mind only wants to talk to the higher self, it is quite achievable to do this and not hear what other spirits are trying to tell you.

When the human mind focuses on the body and ignores the higher self, they shut out all aspects of the universe. Their body will be aligned and therefore able to heal physical wounds but they will not be able to, or rather have more difficulty connecting with the Total or All there **is.**

When the human mind uses a meditation technique that takes the focus away from the self and centers on other beings, healing can be done for others but how much will be achieved by self? Of course, we are talking about someone who completely disconnects from the needs of the self. Yes, this is very selfless and at times a good objective. However when a soul enters the Earth Plane, the soul, in some aspects, is selfish because he/she wants to achieve all their own goals so they can return to the Total. With this thought in mind, trying to help all the other souls on the Earth Plane except your own, does not help your individual soul. Helping other souls is good and should be done, but the main work should be done by the souls who are waiting to come down to the Earth. This does not mean, and we want to stress, that all humans should ignore others and be entirely selfish. Not so, we are only saying that when the human goes into a meditation, the objective should be centering for the personal soul and not for the purpose of others alone.

Some meditation methods also try to blank the mind completely. This is a very good method to be used in combination with the other methods. By blanking your mind, you will miss the connection with the spirit guides who are trying to work with you and help you complete your learning.

You have often spoken of the meditation that is achieved while out with the trees. This is the best method of healing a human can use because all nature has the energies that are needed by the human to heal.

Until the human evolves to a dimension where they can travel and move to other dimensions, forms and planets, we recommend a blend of meditation or centering techniques. Mix

- *some for higher self connection, ignoring the physical*
- *some for the body alone*
- *some for all others and*
- *some blanking*

When these are combined, the human soul and spirit will achieve a balance that it needs. By calling it centering, the spirit can go into all these states and work on whichever goal the soul needs at that time.

All your religious leaders were accurate but with limitations. Each one took one aspect of meditation or centering and taught it to those around him according to what was needed at that time. What was missed was the memory that some of the knowledge is passed from gene to gene in families and cultures. Later as the physical body evolved, the original purpose was not the only method needed. But, when centering is put in the concept of religion, humans follow it without questioning and will miss the evolution of centering to include other facets of the technique.

We are not saying that you should walk away from your religions and their methods. We are saying, add to them and question what is being passed down to you. Listen when we try to give you information or let us know the best method to be used. Go with our love for now and stay centered and therefore in balance.

It is interesting to learn from our historians that evidence from past centuries proves that humans can live 2-300 years. The development and advancement of civilization may have given us comfort and technology but it also gave us stress and less desire to live long lives.

Meditative Techniques

For those who are curious about the differences between some of the meditative traditions, the following is a brief summary of some of the more popular methods. These summaries come from Daniel Goleman's book *The Meditative Mind.* [2]

---

[2] Goleman, Daniel, *The Meditative Mind*, Putnam Publishing Group, New York, 1988

Hindu Bhakti: This is the strongest school of religious practice in Hinduism. Any object of devotion can be chosen. The purpose of the practice is to keep the thought of the deity foremost in this mind. The Bhakti uses a mala, or rosary as a technical aide. The Bhakti ends in a **quest for the self** — a major difference between Buddhism, which seeks to dissolve the sense of self, and Hindu paths, which aim at **uniting** the seeker with a 'higher' self.

Jewish Kabbalah: They believe that the normal human man is incomplete. He lives a mechanical life, bound by the rhythms of his body, his ego and habitual reactions and perceptions. Kabbalism encourages mankind to observe his ego and become aware of the unconscious self that drive his thoughts and actions. One of the steps to reaching the higher state is to get to know himself through rigorous self-observation. While the rules for their meditation are secret teachings and not available to the public, we do know that they are an offshoot of the normal prayers of the devout Jew. This encourages the participant to center on a single subject.

Christian Hesychasm: Their meditation practices and rules were similar to the Hindu and Buddhist monks. They focus on **selfless love of others.** Their prayers are based on the Bhakti with the rosary, and the Kabbalah with their repetition of a word or phrase. They believed that the only way to overcome sense consciousness is to attain a **silent mind.**

Sufism: Meditation is used as a way to purify the novice's efforts to purify his heart. The main meditation is *zihr,* which is a solitary meditation, starting oral and changing to silent as the study progresses. They use dance, or whirling motion to reach higher states of consciousness. Another goal is to make meditation a way of life for every waking moment.

Transcendental Meditation (TM): This has been described as "a classic Hindu mantra meditation in a modern Western package." Maharishi avoided the use of Sanskrit terms and used scientific findings to validate meditation. Their goal was union of the seeker's mind with the formless Brahma or infinite consciousness, a step beyond the Bhakti's goal of union with a form of God. One way to avoid duality (of God and self) was through the use of a mantra or sound. Even though mantras are meant to be kept secret, we know that all those in similar categories such as age or education are given the same mantra.

Patanjali's Ashranga Yoga: Yoga meditation is acknowledged as being one of the sources of modern Indian meditation system. These spiritual schools include: Bhakti Yoga — path of devotion, Karma Yoga — selfless service, and Gyana Yoga — intellect as the tool. All these seek to achieve the duality through union as we discussed in number 1, Hindu Bhakti. Their goal is to bridge the gap between experiencer and the devotional object They use rigorous discipline of mind and body, including sitting in the lotus position to reach a meditative state.

Indian Tantra: A highly developed magical/mystical religion. Through meditation, spells, posture and symbolic designs they teach the initiate to unlearn time and space so they can unite with the higher self.

Kundalini Yoga: This school of yoga concentrates on the kundalini energy at the base of the spine and takes it up the spine through the seven chakras. Each chakra has attitudes, motives and mental states. The first three chakras, root/survival, second/sexual, and third/persuasion and manipulation of others, are earthly or lower focus. The higher chakras are the heart (fourth) for selfless love, care of others, and compassion, fifth/speaking the truth, sixth/third eye, vision beyond 3-D, and the seventh/crown, beyond physical identity. These last three open us to transcendental states. Kundalini desires to move the energy up to the higher chakras where higher consciousness is attained. Techniques include mantras for visual exercises, inner sounds and controlled ritualistic movement.

Tibetan Buddhism: This is a blend of classical Tibetan and Tantraism. A follower seeks to gain **love and compassion** for all. Their goal is to gain enlightenment for the salvation of all Earth beings. They work on freeing themselves of 'ego' so that they can return to the world and help others. All schools of Tibetan Buddhism center on basic meditative skills of concentration and insight. How they move to advanced skills varies amongst the schools.

Zen: Zen starts with concentration not unlike other methods. A beginner's meditation may focus on breathing. Once the meditator has achieved concentration, they are then given a personal puzzle or *koan* to solve during mediation. They return to this koan whenever the mind wanders. They desire to look into one's own mind, neither despising nor cherishing the thoughts that arise." Their goal is to reach silence within, and not communicate with spiritual world.

Gurdjieff's Fourth Way: This meditation does not involve solitary meditation but instead works on the directing his attention to self-observation through mirror of his relationships with people and things. He can almost be in a trance in his normal day as he focuses on one aspect of his being. For example, he may decide on a particular day to focus on the movement of his hands or facial gestures.

Krishnamurti's choiceless awareness: Krishnamurti did not advocate meditating, either with repetition or stillness. He believed that all thoughts and imagining must be released and the mind empty. He advocates observing without naming.

Meditative Energy

For those who have studied meditation and energy work may feel this section is redundant. When my spirit guides presented this information, it made me remember how easy it is to assume the obvious and forget those who are not familiar with internal energy. It is also useful as a gentle reminder for those who are using it regularly.

We have spoken a great deal about meditation and its importance for healing. What we did not discuss at that time was what is and how does the energy work.

Meditation is a method of healing the body as we have said. You, as humans, tend to think of healing yourselves as only coming from sleeping and slowing down. That is not always so. A sluggish digestive, a sluggish heart does not need slowing down, rather they need to be sped up. So the body will learn to recognize the difference and will call upon what it needs. As we have told you, we, when not in light form, move very slowly. We do move very fast when needed.

The meditation methods you described are all designed to slow the body down. when the mind and spirit are already slow, you may need to speed the energy. During a meditation, you can call in guides to bring in lots of activity. This may be like active dreaming. It can be a learning time to discover how fast movement and events can be. Many of you have sped up vibration and energy around you through active thoughts.

Let us explain in more detail. If you are feeling sluggish and not too active, you take a long time to get things done. Combined with looking at the food you eat, pick colors and stones that vibrate faster. Go into a meditation holding these colors and stones, or place them around you. Slow your breathing to relax and then ask that, in a relaxed state, you be shown a faster vibration. Do this daily for about a week and you will start to notice a change. You should then practice without the colors and stones as support to feel the same effect.

With our help, you will have learned to adjust the vibration according to your needs. You have an expression amongst your people, "fight or flight." When you are in this situation, you have sped up your vibration by altering your metabolism. This can be very important in balancing your body, mind and spirit. This Vibrational Meditation Altering Method connects these three better than some other methods.

Again, as we said about the different meditation methods, you need to recognize when it is appropriate for each one. You need to recognize when you need this method also. When your body is recovering from an invasion whether surgery or virus, the body needs to slow down to heal and speed up to get back into balance at the end. Think of it like a pendulum on a clock. You stop the clock to fix it. You speed it up to get it going again; then you adjust the weight to bring the pendulum into a center motion. Centering, not meditation!

It is very important to get your energies aligned. As you become lined up, then you will be able to move forward to the fourth Dimension as the Mayan require for the end of their millennium. Only those who are aligned will be able to get on the "ARK". Those who do not, will truly have the end of the earth/life as is predicted. This is why it is so important to get the information out so that it will give those who see the light, time to balance their energies with the areas they live in. As each region will send forth people, this will enable the new world to have a balance of energies similar to the earth's today. You have a wide range of energies based on the climate and regions of the earth. Your new world will need the same mix. Depending on the numbers from each region that become 4D (move to the fourth dimension) entities, will determine the success and balance of the new world. This is why LUKE did not want his writings to be given to others in his lifetime. Humans would not understand the concept of 4D, other life forms and would distort it for their use and thereby destroy the future of your culture.

*Mayans were around at the time of LUKE. They influenced LUKE, Jesus and the disciples. Unfortunately, as PAUL has stated, the disciples did not understand the message. Jesus in having to revert to miracles to get people to listen, also made an error because the people still did not get the message. The **Pleiadian** culture made a decision to delay moving your culture forward when they realized how unprepared we were. Now is the time that you have to make a move. After 2012, there will not be a second chance!*

This is very much a premonition of what is to come. It also refers to information that I was given a month before I began to channel this text. The following is the main information from this sitting. It was never revealed to me as to whether Luke was the disciple or not. I did not feel it was important so I have never asked. I do know that the Luke who channels through me is an extremely strong, yet gentle and loving entity

I went back to an arid time, clay houses and lots of noise. There was a man speaking from a platform with crowds gathered. I was a woman, named **LEA** and therefore had to stay at the back. There was a great deal of peace and calm in the square when he spoke. I had blonde hair and was about 22. Luke had been a friend of the family and part of my life for many years. We were nothing more than friends. He was very strong, physically, emotionally and spiritually. He knew what he believed and where he was going. It took a lot to sway him. The first time we were together in the regression was on a hill in a meadow. He expressed his opinions, not to much to teach or sway me but simple conversation.

Later we were on a ship. There were many people, almost as if we were all running away. Next we landed at a beach with a hill rising right from it. I remember climbing the hill and LUKE picking plants. He had many friends. We, more he, made a conscious decision not to become romantically involved. His life involved more important things and he didn't want to be distracted. We both loved each other but I respected his decision and we remained friends. Even though I was a woman he let me be part of the inner circle but I couldn't talk or share my opinions. I also had to keep quiet about the events when talking to other people.

Later, as we grew older he was teaching me all he knew and I was writing it down. It was important that it be recorded for people to come. He didn't trust any of his male friends because they might turn it around and use it for other uses. It turned out that I wrote everything and he printed much under his name. Also much had to be put in a secret place for the future generations. Luke talked and wrote about the way of life and health and ways to heal yourself and others.

Tranquility is the key to a long life. Have you ever seen or heard about spirits that were moving quickly and rushing. We all take life slowly. The same things can be accomplished with serenity and peace as you can accomplish rushing. Rushing, it actually takes longer. We spirits who live on other planes and dimensions do not need to move quickly. By increasing our vibration, we are still tranquil and serene. A higher vibration will allow you to process more information but still at a slower pace. This is hard for us to describe because you have a limited concept of what options are open to you. What we can tell you now is — slow down. By slowing down and not getting so excited, you will open other dimensions and build your DNA strands faster.

It is the one guaranteed way to create peace in your world. Unfortunately, most of your beings move quickly and are impatient. This is one reason what you have not been well for the past two days. You want to accomplish too much too fast. When someone comes to you for help, use only one tool and keep the time short. It is not a matter of not being giving. It is a matter of bringing about a slowness in both you and the person who needs help.

Rushing and moving quickly seems to be the only option open to humans at this time. We have never experienced a higher vibration, so it is difficult to understand that we can achieve more, move faster and enjoy more, if we simply slow down. Unfortunately, civilization and industry do not understand at this time.

The last sentence appears disconnected to the rest of the passage. It refers to helping others. Often we are helping more by helping less. Appearing calm and disconnected from individuals may be the most help we can give. When they observe and absorb, they will bring the calmness and peace into themselves.

Reiki, or hands on healing is one method of achieving this. and why it is becoming so popular. For you and your knowledge, it is a way to demonstrate that it works. We will help you select the best method for each person at that particular time.

Hands-on healing is becoming more and more important in the Western world. One of the reasons is that it is a restful way to bring healing into our body. Most hands-on healing allows the body to move into a meditative state that is healing by itself.

The key to health is to balance the energies of your body to those around you. This means living according to the area that you live in. When you meditate, or center, regularly and walk in nature, you are slowing your body down enough to read the energy of the environment. This is the key to your body balancing the energy within.

According to Ayurveda [and this can be applied to ANY area of the world], there are three main energy systems in our body. They are set at the time we are born, usually according to your locale. By using the right foods and right herbs, we can keep them balanced [the energy systems]. Nature helps us keep them synchronized. When we do not read the energies of nature, we have a much bigger job of keeping our internal energy systems in balance. Living a full and complete life allows us to keep them balanced with a minimum of effort.

Harmonizing our energy with nature does not have to include studying the energies or metabolism of the body. Indigenous people around the world connect with nature and often making this the focus of their living. We think of ourselves as being superior to all other life on Earth. However, all living creatures listen and communicate with all aspects of nature, becoming one. Birds listen and use nature to help them avoid their hunters. Plant life learns when to grow or when to rest, saving its energy for a later time. We could learn so much from them. Read on!

Animals*. Animals have a definite energy pattern. Cats are faster, dogs are calmer. When you see a fast/hyper dog, the energy within is still slow even though they appear fast. The same with cats. People* *talk about cats being calming but in fact, they have a faster energy. The ones that are most important are birds. I am talking about wild birds. Their energy is very calm and centering. When you see a bird flying, they help bring your energy into the center to align with the nature around you. Fish, since they are usually white/tan in color, are more neutral.*

Energy should be lined up like focusing a camera. If the lines are not uniform, the picture is blurry So it is with the energy of the earth, universe and body...all must be lined up.

Desert/arid/hotter climates will have a more neutral → moving to a faster energy. Then humans would pay attention to the sunset, moon, season to help balance the energy.

When we live in the desert or hotter climate, we need to focus on sunrises and sunsets for balance. We should avoid looking at a bright red sunset as this will increase the vibration within us and we will not sleep well that night.

Seasons are also energy dependent. Winter is white and therefore neutral, spring and fall more green. Summer, while there is more green around has more of a red nature. This is partly due to the colors of the flowers. Most colors have a red component to them, making them a faster energy.

In the previous section, I indicated that we should not look at a red sunset. However, in the Winter, this causes less agitation than during the hot summer months.

Anger *Anger does not come from outside influence. It is an imbalance of the energies within. Next time you get mad, or someone near you, look at what would cause an imbalance of their energies. Have they moved? Have they eaten different foods? Has their lifestyle changed? All these will shift the imbalance and will cause an increase [or decrease] in one of the energies. When something outside happens, it then increases the one energy beyond a normal range and triggers anger. The same thing applies with many of the 'emotional' diseases that are around today. What you call bi-polar is nothing more than an imbalance that has gone on for a long time. People should look at the lifestyle of the sick person and how it has changed over the past several years. The amount of change will vary from one person to another. Each person has his/her own limit. Also they must look at the buildup of imbalances. They may be able to accept one imbalance and readjust their systems but several may be too much. The more imbalances, the more our DNA will go out of balance and we will end up using fewer strands.*

You are all made up of the energy as we have talked about. The freer you are in spirit and in physical being, the lighter you will be and therefore the more energy you will have. It is important to remember that this freedom is not only real but also in perception. If you do not consider yourselves free, then you will be burdened with heavier energy. It is almost impossible to match heavy energy with that of nature (your earth) and the universe. One way to keep yourselves light is to use laughter. The more laughter, the lighter, or more space around the energy fields within you. It is important that people remember, or learn, how to chew Jell-O. A room full of people chewing Jell-O is one way of reminding people that they do not laugh as much as they should. Jell-O reminds us of the simpler things in life and how just being silly is beneficial.

Society has placed a 'right' way of behaving. Chewing Jell-O does not conform.

When you do not perceive yourselves as being free, or, in reality are not, the energy is more compact and also thicker and tougher.

The heavier energy is what manifests anger and violence. Love is the key to keeping us light and therefore free. It is difficult to give love to ourselves and others when we are fighting to keep our energy compact, thick and tough. Protection is given to ourselves when we expand our **aura,** or energy field. This is almost always light energy. A comparison is the spider web. It is light and filmy and yet is one of the strongest fields that nature provides.

Organic, is another way of getting lighter energy. It is also another way of getting energy that will match your region where you live. Chemicals will be made in a different region and will not conform to your area.

Organic lightens the energy within the body. When we feel lighter within, we are able to put more love into our outer energy field and to others.

It is extremely important that people on your planet slow down. This is not only the pace of living but the *energy within. You cannot be prepared to move forward with your beings [human beings as a race] until you slow down. You must also learn to consciously slow down the energy within your body. There are a few times when you may need to speed it up but generally, you need to live at a slow pace. Unfortunately, people took to riding horses and other creatures. This sped your energy up. It gave you the information but you didn't learn to use it **only** when you needed faster energy to move quickly from one place to another. By speeding up and using this all the time, you generated an anger that resulted in wars. If you had stayed at a slower/lower energy, wars would not have resulted. At the time when you lived before, people did get angry and greedy but if they had been willing to accept our knowledge, they would have learned to accept others for who they are and living at a slower, loving pace. Most of your religions today offer the same belief. They do not say to live slow specifically but they do recommend meditating/praying , eating slowly, not eating as must [eating for pleasure and allowing the body to absorb it] and going out into nature. All this will slow the energy down. Plus, they recommend staying in one place.*

This passage gives some key points worth emphasizing.

> 1: Meditation and centering, bio-feedback, soft martial arts and yoga are all methods of slowing down your internal speed.

2: Single horses and other modes of transportation should be used only if you **must** move from location to location, not as a way of life.

3: You cannot move from the present dimension until you learn to slow down the living and energy emitted to others.

4: Now that society has the information needed to advance and improve technology, we can take the time to observe and absorb information at a slower pace. This does not include television and radio. It refers to information from nature and channeled information.

5: It is difficult to give love when you are moving at a fast pace. **Love** does not travel at high speed.

6: High speed produces anger.

*Unfortunately, Christians when they do go into other regions do so for the wrong reason. They go to convert and insist others convert their beliefs, lifestyle and eating habits. They should instead help them live a good, gentle life. They should help them learn how to grow crops **according** to their climate and region, not what they think they should eat. They should teach them to read. Unfortunately, the reading is only to read the religious text. Christians seem to be the only religion that thinks this is a must. Other religions do not push the same way. It is because the religion is* *broken off into small groups. This occurred even when Jesus was preaching. His followers, all got a different message and they felt it was right. The truth is out there but you will never find it because all insist theirs is the **right** one.*

Jesus was stressing the importance of loving one another. He should have stressed the importance of loving yourself. By loving yourself, you will slow down. When you are calmer and more at peace, others will seek you out and then you can live your lifestyle. Unfortunately, there is not the time now to take that approach. People must slow down their energy personally, be more selfish because there is not enough time left to all people to see the importance and benefit of your way of life.

It is important to understand that is not Christianity itself that is being attacked. Attacking is far from the objective. Jesus was an enlightened being who came to Earth and gave us one of the best messages possible. Unfortunately, the greed and desire of the human race influenced all around him. The world was not ready for the lessons and messages that were coming to Earth. Other races also fell under this influence. The Mayan, Egyptian, Incas also felt this influence. Mankind started out as a race from another planet. They started out with the challenge of learning about emotion. Unfortunately, Spirits and other beings who tried to help with the learning, did so too early in the life of the world. Today, individuals must trust their instincts and realize that society, the leaders and the corporations are fighting to hold onto their power. through fear. Individuals do not need this form of power. If we, as humans, learn to trust and realize our power, we will have more power than was ever thought possible. Releasing the power, gives all of us the ability to **love** ourselves and all creatures. With this Love, the capability of speeding up our vibration, moving to a higher vibration, traveling the universe and galaxy becomes within our reach. We have only to trust and believe that we do not need the power as perceived by humans on this planet.

For centering, you need scents that are soft and feminine. This will differ from some of the books but always ask yourself, is it gentle and feminine? If not, it will bring in the mental. The scent we give you when we are around is an example. The burnt toast is not the writer of the book. It is spirit energy that will direct you and set you on the path, but not the writing. This is the gentleness of SHAYLA. Luke, or Illusions will do the healing. Yes, you should be doing more, but you need to develop the habit of a writing routine and then you can get back into healing.

My spirit guides spoke many times of aromas and the power within them. There are many writings that talk of the power of gentle aromas. I receive one of two aromas when my guides want to talk to me. One is a very soft, delicate perfume. The other one does smell like someone is burning the toast in the kitchen! Again I refer the reader to one of the many books on aromatherapy for selecting the aroma right for you. I also encourage you to go with your instincts rather than what the book says if there is a conflict between the two.

The movement of the energy is most important in the body. When performing a Reiki, the energy waves should be visualized as moving very slow, almost slow motion. Try to see them as moving in a fluid, musical movement throughout the body.

When bringing in the colors of the chakras, bring them in through the crown and then see them parallel in the body, moving down beside one another and moving in unison..dancing. This is a way to get a feel of the energy and what it should look like wherever you live, desert or forest.

The Spirit world chooses things or examples that are familiar to us as examples of their message. There are many energy systems in this world, but the energy system that is most familiar to me is Reiki. Therefore, they used this method so that I would be able to fully understand the principle.

You came up with a comparison of riding the waves or tides to describe the balance that must occur in your bodies. This is also useful for looking at the entire world/universe energy. **Unless the energies are balanced and in sync, there is stress on all systems.** *The ecosystem must have that match. Farmers lost sight of the balance when they start to combine nutrients to get a bigger growth. They should be careful with what they combine. Nutrients added to address the food shortage only causes violence and unrest in different communities.*

Unfortunately, we are only starting to understand this balance. For example, in an effort to increase output, nutrients are added at the expense of the root system. The farmers and scientists rationalize that the plants are pulled up at the end of the year and new crops are planted in coming years, therefore, roots are not important. What is forgotten is that the root system feeds the earth and micro-life around it. When the roots are starved, so is the entire system surrounding the plant.

Nutrients to increase food output are usually selected for the plant growth only and the transfer to the consuming human is ignored. These nutrients are chemicals foreign to the human body.

Ripples. *There are so many ripples in your life, whether they be in clouds, water, or energies around us. You spend so much time trying to smooth them out when it is not really necessary. What is a ripple but a variety in the regular life? Can you imagine how boring life and all around you would be if everything was smooth with no variation? You all need variation and variety. It is important to realize that the variety must be a match of your energy of yourselves and the energy around you. This means that a trip to another region does not constitute a good variety. It will be challenging to take that energy and blend it into what is around you. Variety, as part of where you live, is a calming and soothing type.*

*There is a saying in your world that says you should live in the present or **now**. That is fine but it is also important to either do one of two things. Make the* *now **s-o-o** small that we cannot see the ripples on the edge or else make the **now** so big that the ripples look so small that they are not important. It depends on how you look at life as how each person looks at the ripples.*

Ripples also have a silver lining if you look at them for a short time. Silver linings bring joy. They are cooling and balancing at the same time as being energizing.

When you look at a tree or other life form, they are also ripples in varying sizes. If you look at a feather, it is like looking at a ripple so small that you can't see the edges. If you look at bird in the distance, the ripple is so small that it is unimportant. However, if you look at the wing when it is in flight and at a close range, the wing can look very disorganized and you might worry about whether it will fly. A mother trusts the baby and doesn't see the ripple but rather the big bird. Peace comes with both the big overview and the small microscopic vision. For you in this world, it is important to take the big picture and enjoy. You are in life form of a human this time so that you can learn to view the ripples from the best perspective. Remember that when you buried the papers so long ago, you were looking at the big ripple. You knew that the papers would not get lost and be torn by people looking at a smaller view. It is time to focus on completing what you have and get it published so that the papers can be found.

The last part of this passage is a personal note to me. The remainder is for all who read it. This passage is very clear and can be applied to any situation facing any person at any time. Therefore, I ask the reader to select what is important for them.

Again, keep your body in balance within itself.

Keep your body in balance with the region you live in and/or were born in.

Give help according to the needs of those by who receive it.

Don't try to convert. Give the spiritual help helping them remember to look after their spiritual peace, not do what you think is best. People who are receiving, if they are fairly well balanced, will return to the center of their being after a short, minor jerk to either the left or right.

This is an excellent summary passage. You will find this repeated many times throughout the book. We, as humans tend to forget what is either unpleasant or requires work on our part. Balancing should not be difficult but does require modifying our life styles and thought process.

There is an old adage that you should always give gifts that you would like to receive yourself. It is an excellent idea but not always practical. If I liked cut crystal and purple and you liked stoneware dishes and hated purple, it would not be appropriate to give you something that I liked. For the same reason, sending winter clothing to someone living in the tropics is also not appropriate.

This same principle applies to giving on a spiritual level. There are many paths to spiritual peace and the Total, All there is, God, or whatever name is applied.

Imbalance, turmoil, and self-doubt will grow exponentially once an idea that is perceived as wrong is introduced into a society. In the industrial world, this is also called stress. In the spiritual world, this is called disaster. The last passage in this section talks about Friday the 13th and full moons. For many cultures and belief systems, these are important. We do know that the magnetic energy for a full moon is more powerful.

Friday the 13th. *This is the day that everything should start rolling out. It is important that people be aware of the impact of this day in the present year. It is a date when those who have started to becoming balanced will become even more balanced. For you, it is a time to remain very quiet and focus on your balancing. Those who are working close with you should also do the same. Sit out under the moon and absorb the energy. If you have a group who can perform a ceremony on this date, do so. It is important that you get balanced at this time and absorb whatever energy the moon can give you. Spend as much of the day out of doors go pick up the energy of nature. Eat pure on this day and you will want to eat pure thereafter. This will be a turning point for you. You will receive the information you need at that time. Those with you will also receive information. It will be a time of sadness for some but remember that a great birth will happen shortly after. It has to fall to come back up again. Rewards are greatest after a fall.*

In a later channeling, I was assured that the sadness and 'fall' are not major disasters. They are more of self-discovery where there is little chance to return to old patterns. The next section on our **Food Connection** talks about eating light or heavy depending on the moon pattern. Again, I would like to remind you that all connections are best combined.

Using Food for the Connection

Should you scan ahead, you may become overwhelmed about the amount of detail in this chapter. Again, I want to emphasize that the ideas be taken one at a time and take the idea or recommendation that appeals to you the most. If you tried to change your living pattern all at once, this would create stress for the body. **That is not being in balance!** Food is probably one of the most important things that we can do for our body, mind and spirit, simply because our lives are centered around eating. Why? It doesn't matter what genetic patterns you carry through your family. It doesn't necessarily matter who your social connections are. What does matter is that that over the millenniums, humans have altered their eating habits to bring an easier lifestyle and to conform to the social pressures. This latter can be as simple as traditional banquets or it can be as damaging as eating to gain acceptance. Rather than fight social or family pressure, go along with it and make small changes. Soon, those around you will want to know more and then you can smile and gently explain.

When the soul is ready to search for balance bringing peace to the human being, selecting the right food is probably the best point to begin the search.

A great deal is being talked about in this book about the need to stay in the locale where you reside. This is valid for several reasons. First, the soul chose to enter a body vibrating at a certain rate according to the place of residence. Second, the food contains the nutrition that your particular body requires. Many may question food as being so important. Yes, they know that the food nutrients are essential for the physical body and, yes, stimulants are damaging to the mind. However, connecting the spirit, mind and body does not seem as readily apparent as the other factors.

When our spirit decides to enter a body and live on the Earth Plane, it is vibrating at a universal rate. It will slow down or alter its frequency in order to enter and fit the physical body. These adjustments are made according to the Earth as a whole plus the location where the soul is prepared to live. The soul, each time it comes to Earth, agrees to live in a certain time, in a certain location, in a certain body. All three move at a certain speed. Anything that alters this speed, puts pressure and strain on the physical body and, more importantly, on the spirit or soul as it tries to accomplish the tasks that it set out to complete.

To us, the human body is extremely complex and advanced. But it is really a very primitive part of the universe. Unlike other energies in the universe, this body cannot modify its energy patterns readily. On the Earth Plane, it requires many centuries to alter the genetics of the body. We impose bodily pressure with our air travel around the world. We also increase the stress and strain by including food that do not meet the physical needs of the body **as it was decided at birth.**

As humans, we have a responsibility to adjust our life style to return our body to a balance state. It is only then that our body, mind and spirit can reside in peace. These three are losing their connection and we need to rebuild the bridges. Food is one tool that can help us achieve this goal.

The Energy of Food

When this topic is mentioned, most individuals think in terms of calories, the burning power of food. This is not the definition for the purpose of this book. For us, energy is defined as the vibrational rate as it pertains to the planet and the universe. This allows us to become part of the universal population. Calories do not give us this. Calories are for the physical body alone. They allow the body to operate as a machine. **Our** energy allows us to operate as our soul is intended. There is a great difference.

Most of your people do not recognize the importance of food energy. All food carries the energy from where it came. It is one of the strongest connections you can have. This is why it is so important to take care of your planet. When the earth is abused and polluted, you will see the sadness and irritation come through. Today, most of it will be balanced by humans through other means, music, fire and color. However, it won't be long before this will be impossible. There will be too much for either the planet or human to handle. Since you do not grow your own personal food as in the past, you have to rely on others. Of course, knowing who grew it is best.

Cleansing with smudge and healing when you get it home is the second best. Last is running your hand over your food silently while asking for good energy from us (the spirits) to be put back in. We do our best. However, when food carries the anger and sadness of the Earth, the farmer, the market and delivery people, we can only do so much.

This is a time for individuals to make their wishes known. Few bother to check out where food comes from. You may feel proud that you check whether it is organic or from your region; but do you take the time to find out who harvested it? Were they at the mercy of a big business farmer? Was it slave labor? Were they ill from not getting enough nutrition? Each of you have the responsibility to stop the unfairness. By helping others and sending love, you will help to balance the energy that comes from our food. Do not forget that all injustices from all parts of the food chain is transferred to your food.

Root foods will carry pain that is felt in the Earth only. Stem food will have both the Earth and Air. Fruits will carry more of the air injustice. This can be the remains of Earth's pain, but it will also carry energy shifts picked up from the auras or energy fields of all that pass by, plus the pollutants in the air.

Many on your Earth Plane have studied auras and their colors for the purpose of healing the body that carries it. Not many have looked, or accepted what this does to others who are nearby. It is acknowledged that the people pollutants are felt, such as being in room full of angry people. However, the impact of ALL life is not there.

You just asked what a person can do if they live in a city, do not have time to heal their food but want to do as much as possible. Cleaning foods and eating as raw as possible will keep the energy from being overrun by the cooking energy. Eating foods as fresh as you can get. Going out into nature regularly and silently talking to plants and asking permission to consume their brothers. The plants do not have to be the same, although that is best.

We have talked about fast and slow foods and the speed of food colors. Match the speed with your body. Learn whether you are fast or slow when you are in good health and learn to read your body when you are not in good health. You can then consume foods to bring back the energy of your good health.

The majority of the people I know do not feel that they can do anything about what goes on beyond their personal world. This is not so. We can make our feelings heard. We can take the time to find out who supplies our foods. We can look at the integrity of corporations. It is not difficult to gather information but it does take time and you do have a choice. If you choose to accept the food as it is presented then it is important that you bring the energy of the foods to match your body as best you can. They gave us three ways of do this.

1. Learn who grew your food and where it came from.

2. Cleanse with smudge or similar technique as soon as you bring the food home. They are assuming that you are washing with pure water.

3. Slowly run your hand over your food before consumption.

For busy city people:

1. Cleansing and eating foods as fresh and raw as feasible.

2. Balancing yourself by walking in nature after your meals.

These last two suggestions are not beyond any one person's achievement. When they are not followed, it is because someone is looking for an excuse. Read on for more solutions and information.

It Must be Food to Feed the Spirit

Eat and plant according to lunar cycle. When moon is full, eat light. New moon, eat heavy. Energy transmitted by the moon is more concentrated and active. As moon becomes full, this has more impact on energy of the body.

According to the Ayurvedic knowledge of life cycles and energy, this is even more valid. The moon is considered to be cool, slow and dense. This time will aggravate the energies of the body that share these properties. By eating light, warm foods, the energy concentration is reduced. The concentration of fluids in the body are also the highest at full moon.

Therefore, you want to include foods that will not increase the liquid in the body.

At the new moon, there is minimal energy coming from the moon so we need to increase the energy consumed so that our body will stay in balance.

We need to remember that the triad — body, mind, spirit — work best when they are in balance for each individual.

Larger fruit means more water, energy and food in each fruit.

When we need more fluid in our bodies, this is when we should consume large fruit, such as grapefruit, melons. When we need to reduce the fluid or energy, fruits such as kiwi, bananas or apples are best.

Green is a slow energy. Any fruit or vegetable that is green is slower and will help to balance the earth energy around you. You may need to eat green to balance or you may need red or yellow ... white is neutral. The energy you are around or consume will help you become more in balance with the surrounding energy.

Prior to your personal meditation, it is recommended that you eat something that is green as well as surrounding yourself with green; one more reason to meditate outside in the green fields. If you are feeling slow and sluggish, try eating red or yellow fruit. You will find you will get more energy and become more creative. These last two colors should not be held when you are about to meditate.

Another way to utilize color is to have jars of each color near. Place a gelatinous sheet of the appropriate color around a jar of pure, distilled water. Place this jar in the sunlight for approximately 4 hours. The water will absorb the properties of the color. This can be taken internally if you are not able to absorb green, red or yellow any other way.

Olives will ease stress and help you accept what you cannot change. Black olives are wake-up. Good for people who always feel tired. Pimento is not recommended when they are the center of green olives.

When we are under stress, we cannot think clearly, nor can we connect with the spirits. When we honor our body by staying calm, then we are able to meditate and think clearly.

Chocolate is another word that I have been sending to you throughout the day. What does it mean to you? Think about the sound, the feeling, the taste and you will answer the question yourself.

It is gratifying and will awaken the most inner senses of your being. There are other foods that do the same but chocolate is the most popular with people in your lifetime.

Chocolate was esteemed by the Incas, Mayans, and Aztecs for its energizing properties. Unfortunately, in Western society, it has been given a bad reputation. It is still a great comfort food, whether it is solid chocolate or a warm cup of hot chocolate. Therefore, when you feel slow, tired and listless, a small piece of chocolate (or cup) will awaken the body, stimulate the mind and yet, calm the spirit. It does have a high fat content so we emphasize the word **small.**

*Watermelon and other fruit, even though not a part of your region are good for you because they get the individual body used to eating fruit. Watermelon is a way to get **natural** water into the system. Fruit is the best type of food to eat. When it is consumed properly, it is not necessary to worry about protein.*

The best fruit, of course, is organic and preferably grown in your region. If this is not a possibility, then buy your fruit, ripe and as good a quality as possible. If the fruit is organic, then the body can tolerate food from another region and will assimilate it into your body's energy system.

Fruit is best eaten at the beginning of the meal to ensure that is digested first. This minimizes the fermentation time in the acidic stomach, therefore increasing the benefits that the body receives from the nutrients. All melons are high in Vitamin A and C. As the channeled information mentions, watermelon will get natural water into the system. This fluid is pure and lacks the chemicals of civilization. India has used watermelon for over 4000 years.

The channeled information also talks about not worrying about protein. Usually, people who listen to their body include nuts and grains in their daily diet. It is interesting to note that while fruit is still low on protein, melons have the highest protein of all the fruit families. If you are eating a mainly fruit diet, it is not difficult to get 20 grams of protein in a day. (This is the recommended amount of many nutritionists). A small handful of nuts or grains gives you what is missing.

The nuts and grains will give you the necessary protein. People on your planet are complaining about allergies, nuts being one of them. They are only allergic because they have abused their body. Once they have been off corrupt food and pay attention to their life style, they will be able to eat the foods again. Once a person is confident with the path they are on, all illness will be cleared from the body. This includes cancer, arthritis, high blood pressure. Becoming aware of the illness is a wakeup call to pay attention to the body. People don't bother to listen to the wakeup call and continue to eat poor foods and take drugs as an easy remedy.

Fasting regularly and making a dedicated effort to change your diet to pure, healthy foods can be the first step to cleansing your body of allergies and other illnesses. Don't forget to include pure drinking water!

It is also important to look at the regions and what they offer. The colder, the region, the more a person would want to eat dried fruit and nuts. Grown in the region. Buying locally is the best way to help people. Stay away from herbs that are not grown locally and dried. For some people dried herbs are worse than taking food from a different region. Here testing or asking the body is the way to go. Windows are useful for growing and for converting the water that you harvest. Even the rain is better than what is given to you by the government. Each person can gather rain in their yard and purify it in the window. The desert can use the underground streams to get their water. Fruit will give them the necessary moisture.

Many times during the channeling, it has been stressed that eating foods from where you live is extremely important. The Earth, as does everything around us, vibrates at a certain rate and pattern. When we live in a region, we adapt to this pattern. If we consume food from a different region, and a different vibration, it places stress on our digestion system.

They have mentioned that cold climates need dried nuts. Nuts are warming in action so they will help to warm the body in a cold climate. Dried fruit will swell up when they are eaten and this will also help to warm the body.

In many regions it is difficult to find herbs that are not local. Some simply will not grow in your climate or in a greenhouse. If you choose to include dried herbs, use them in small quantities and make sure that the main part of your food is local.

When they talk about testing or asking the body, scientific testing, muscle checking or dowsing are methods to get reliable answers.

Water is responsible for and involved in nearly every bodily process including digestion, absorption and circulation. It is the primary transporter of nutrients. When we drink water that has chemicals, these chemicals must fight with the nutrients and food for space in the system. Chemicals are usually the winner since they have been produced to be survivors.

In areas where there are **not** a lot of chemicals used on the surface farming, underground streams provide a good source of water. Unfortunately, there are very few areas in the world where the underground streams have remained pure.

Regrettably, in many parts of the world, the rainwater contains the air pollutants but after collecting the water, we can then steam-distill it. This removes inorganic minerals that cells and tissues reject or could cause damage to our body.

Fruit or moist foods contain a large quantity of water. If they are consumed raw or lightly steamed, most of the nutrients are left.

If you meditate regularly, you can trust your inner knowing as to what to eat. Until then listen to the chemists as to what to eat. It is better to combine their knowledge with other information to come up with the ideal menu.

Our bodies know what is needed. Unfortunately, we don't listen often enough. When we pay attention, we will be able to discriminate between cravings for what simply tastes good and what our body **really** needs. When they say listen to the chemists, the recommendation is the type of diet as well as the nutritional components of each food.

If you are learning to listen to your body, it is best to begin with a cleansing regime so that you are listening to a pure song.

Each person should learn how to feel energy so that they know what is going to be good. By feeling the energy around [the body], this sends a message to the body and the body, if in good balance, will be able to adjust more quickly.

When we are sensitive to the energy around and within us, we learn to trust the information we are receiving. There are many energy programs that we can study to develop the reading of our energy. These may include exercise, martial arts, healing arts, scientific equipment. Yoga, Tai Chi, Chi Gong, Reiki and Chi Machines are only a few of the methods.

Cooking with organic oats, spelt flour is better than using the commercial oats or regular flour. There is so much chemicals added that it can cause an imbalance in your body. Spelt will still have some chemical but not as much. Unfortunately, it is grown in a different region so that they will be some imbalance for those living in the northern regions of N.A.

Oats and spelt flour are easier for the body to digest. They also do not have the added chemicals. Durham wheat, which is used in North America, comes from a strain that was developed to withstand the winters.

When eating root vegetables, bring the energy from the earth and practice regularly so that you can move the energy from top or bottom without consciously thinking about it.

As you work with energy and meditation, you can quietly direct the flow from the vegetable and earth through your body. When you slow or vary the speed, this will help you to align the energy to your body. This works for food that comes from trees as well.

It is best to eat them individually so that you can work with the speed of the waves.

Blueberries are one of the best sources of iron and fluid in your diet. Many people dismiss blueberries as being something only mountain people eat. That is not so. While wild are the best for iron and other nutrients, harvested blueberries are still a good source. It is also something that is easily to digest and also provides roughage. Blueberries and chicken are also tasty.

They are assuming organic and from your region of residence.

Corn bread is an excellent staple for all regions. In the northern, moister climates, it can be harvested, ground after drying and then made into corn bread

Maple syrup is not the best to have with corn bread if it doesn't grow in your region. Raspberry syrup or other syrups made from fruits in your region are the best choice.

What they are saying here is that if corn isn't grown naturally in your region, maple syrup will aggravate the balance in your body. There are many syrups or spreads that when combined with the corn bread bring balance to your system.

Also sugar cane is not the best sweetener. Again it is too refined but more importantly, it does not come from your region.

Honey made locally is the best sweetener. Understanding the chemical conversion is important so that you can made alterations in the recipes. Some honeys can be cooked. It depends on the flower where they get the nectar. Wild flowers make the best nectar and can also be combined with local fruit for a syrup.

Most nutrition literature focuses on the refinement of sugar. These scientists feel this is more damaging than being from another region. While refinement is bad, the region of origin is more important when you want to achieve balance. The body, in **small** doses, can handle the chemicals and refinement.

Most nutritionists do not consider honey as providing anything to the body, just as sugars are empty calories. However, honey does have vitamins and minerals that we need. Other foods are a better source of these vitamins and minerals and do not include empty calories. Foods that have a sweet taste can satisfy the sweet tooth without contributing calories. If you want to eat honey, simply because you like the taste, select wild flower, and unpasturized. This honey is more likely to be free from chemicals, unheated, and unrefined. Heating does damage the properties of honey.

All regions of the world can handle and feed the population that is there. There is no need to stop birth.

There are other reasons to control population. However, over time, all regions have adapted their diet to meet the needs of their region or country.

People in the regions must simply understand that they do not need to eat as much and to eat the local food.

Previously it was mentioned that there was ample food on the Earth Plane and there should never be a shortage. To achieve this, we must learn to consume only that fills us. This does not mean eating until we can't swallow another morsel. Nor does it mean eating more than one plateful. When we get in the routine of fasting regularly, we can learn to read our body and we will know what sufficient is and when to stop.

Away back in your history there was scurvy on the ships that started people thinking about oranges. It was not the lack of oranges, it was too much of other foods that caused the imbalance in the diet, causing scurvy. Today, people have learned more but have ignored the idea of applying their new knowledge to old problems and replacing solutions with new, better ones.

This is not saying that our history books were wrong; to the contrary. There was scurvy and people died as a result. This would not have happened if planning had included a diet similar to what people were used to eating on land before setting sail. If citrus fruit was obtainable, this could have been introduced gradually to give those traveling time to adjust to a new energy around them.

One of the best reminders for us is to think back to our grandparents and what we ate when we visited them. We have developed better ways of preserving foods (new solution). However with the introduction of instant and 'fast' foods, we added new problems. I am always reminded of when margarine was introduced. While it is not an ideal food, there were not as many chemicals until they began to color it to make it look like butter.

Cleansing the system is something that is very popular in your new healthy world. It should not be necessary. Simply changing your diet gradually and learning what is right for our body is the best way. Toxins will leave naturally.

People around the world have fasted for various reasons for centuries, some of them spiritual. This information is not saying to stop fasting. Instead, they suggest that eating properly reduces the need for long fasts. A short monthly fast rests our systems and rids itself of toxins. When we eat properly, we will learn to listen to our body and chemicals will be reduced.

Cream cheese is good for you. You should not eat commercial yogurt. Home made with fresh culture is best. Dairy should always be fresh and not made with a lot of chemicals. Regular cheese that your people like is made with chemicals and therefore not good for you. That is why cream cheese is OK. It should not be mixed with pimento but is OK to mix with other foods. Make sure that it is not sour. Again consider the region you live in. Sour is not suitable in dry regions and too much in a rain forest can be difficult to balance. It is useful when you are moving from one region to another. It is a quick balancer. Fresh yogurt can be quick start and when it is combined with local fruit, it is very good for you.

Butter, commercial is also not good for you. Some of you eat Gee. When it is made from commercial butter, it is not good. It is better to find pure milk/cream and make your own butter. Then make the ghee. Margarine is not good at all. There are too many chemicals.

Ghee is the Sanskrit name for clarified butter. The main purpose, again, is to eat foods that are as pure and free from chemicals as possible. When it comes from your region, it will be fresh, better quality and of course, have a compatible energy system.

Eat according to the region you live in. In the Eastern world, they use 5 elements. In other regions, they follow four. Eat according to where you are. Each meal, should contain at least one of each elements at time. It is OK to include two of one but no more. For example. Two root vegetables are OK but not three. If you are not eating fish, then a glass of water will make up the water element. All foods, regardless of where you live, should be soft cooked. This is to kill off any unwanted foods. It may seem to you that the food will be bland but when you learn how to cook, they can be quite good. After all, it is only to keep you alive.

When they refer to unwanted foods, they are referring to bacteria, germs, etc.

The five elements of traditional Chinese medicine (TCM) are: Fire, Earth, Metal, Water, Wood. TCM combines these elements with cold and warm and the seasons. Working with all these, they balance the yin/yang. When choosing to include two, make sure they are in accord with the seasons.

The four elements of Ayurveda are: Air, Fire, Water and Earth. For a healthy lifestyle, Ayurveda combines these with the seasons, age, and temperature. This is called balancing the three *doshas*, or energy systems of the body.

There are many good books available on either system. Some cover more than one health system. If this topic interests you, I recommend selecting a book that deals with only one system.

Storage of foods during the year are best in a freezer or in the ground. It is good to dig a hole in the ground and place tight bags in there. It is sealed with rocks, the unwanted will not get in. Canning is also OK since it will kill off the unwanted. However, there is also the danger of other things living there.

When food is frozen fresh, the energy that was transferred from the Earth to the food will remain in the foods for a period of time. Foods stored underground (root cellar), even though in containers, will still absorb the Earth's energy. In both cases, this energy will be given to whoever eats the food. Canning involves cooking and the cooking destroys living beings and humans will then eat **dead** food.

Green beans and cranberries. A reminder that green vegetables are best. Cranberries are local to your region and therefore good for you.

Both these foods are usually cooked but when they are from your region, and in season, they can be consumed with assurance that your balance and energy will improve.

This piece of channeled is a reminder that we should continually strive to reach higher dimensions that allow us telepathy and moving through time and space.

Green is the color of the heart chakra. When we absorb green and it is pure, we are expanding our compassion and knowledge of relationships, both personal and universal. Red, on the other hand, relates to our personal survival instinct. It is the color of the Root Chakra and gives us courage to fight for what we believe in. When the body and soul are balanced, this fight relates to the survival and contentment of the Total, of which we are a part.

Eat purple grapes with the seeds in it. It is better to eat food as it was created by nature not man. Alterations to food such as removing the seeds for the comfort of the public is not good for the health of the your people.

In present society, we spend so much energy making our life as simple and convenient that we forget what is best for us. Seeds contain all that is needed for birth and growth. By taking seeds out of fruit before we eat, we are removing nutrients essential to our being. When the seeds are removed genetically, the alterations to the product can be very damaging. Unfortunately, we have no idea how this alteration will affect us long term.

Lets look back at wheat. They said that spelt (and kamut) wheat is better for the body. These wheats do not have the bran removed, which is the seed of the wheat. For those who study allergies and their causes, they will know that wheat is one of the biggest causes of allergies in North America.

*Pepper (and this does not apply to all spices) is a useful and necessary spice. When it is put on a dry food and eaten, it will stay dry and not be too hot. However, when it is put or mixed with water, it will expand and become very hot and hard on your system. Think of the mixture as an acid that will burn holes. Dry, it takes longer to become acidic. This is the one time when you are in a moist climate and choose to eat pepper that it is important to consume **a lot** of water with your meal. This will then dilute the spice and prevent burning.*

The premise behind Macrobiotics and Chinese medicine is to keep the foods as alkaline as possible, bringing our stomach's acid into equilibrium. Therefore, we do not want to increase the acid in the system. However, when they say it is useful spice, they are referring to taste. Often foods that are raw or slightly cooked may taste bland. Until your taste buds have adjusted to the new taste, pepper is a simple and effective way to fool your body. When foods are local and fresh, you will surprised at the delight your taste buds will receive. In the meantime, enjoy a small amount of pepper.

Salt is something that your people do not need any longer. Hundreds of years ago it was important, but now your bodies are balanced so that it is not needed. Your body has evolved to the point of not needing it. Iodine is available in the areas of the world where it is necessary. The pores of your skin are open were it is needed

While our bodies do need salt, it is not as important as the media and scientists have led us to believe. We do get enough salt in our foods, through what is given to the food from the earth. Through evaporation of the oceans and this turning to rain on our fields, we get sufficient. Iodine is also available in our foods in sufficient quantities. Salt was added to preserve foods. This is no longer necessary. Salt was added to improve flavor of old food. When we change our diet to include more raw and lightly steamed foods, we will remember the delightful original flavor of foods and salt will no longer be necessary.

Opening the pores for sweating is only necessary in hotter climates. With a clean, balanced body, our pores open more easily and naturally.

*We have tried to show you that there is no need to have food present as you expect to see it. All you had to do was hold out your hand and whatever you needed or any creature who needed nourishment could go there and get what was needed. It was not visible but it was more real than much of the food that is on your world. By placing the essences in the sunlight and asking for a blend of nutrients to be integrated, all essences would have all foods that your people would need. It will take time for your race to accept this because they consider food as a necessary part of living and they could not imagine not sitting down to a meal. However, consider how wonderful it would be if you were able to take a few drops of an essence **before** you go to meet friends and then you could spend all the time and concentration being **with** the person. There* *would be no cooks tired, no worry over money about to be spent and no time chewing. This would be what some of you call quality time.*

To start off, get in the habit of taking an essence first thing in the morning, cut down your breakfast and then taking a different essence before each meal.

*When you make the essence, include things other than the flower. Roots, leaves, vegetables, herbs will all make an essence. You do not always have to have sunlight. A good sun lamp or grow light will give the same energy. You will need to experiment to get the right energy. Again, we stress, stay with what is available in your area. Start in your area and work with other people who are also interested and see what you develop. May we suggest, making an essence out of the same part and use different sources of energy and then see how you feel when you take **each** one.*

This piece of information will be extremely difficult for most people to accept. It will take time. Also, it will probably take several generations for the body to adapt to this type of eating. For us as we evolve, taking an essence blend before each meal and making our own is a wonderful start.

Essences have been used for more than 40,000 years by Aborigines of Australia, Egyptians and other older cultures. However, it wasn't until late 1920s that they were introduced to Western Society by Dr. Edward Bach. Their uses were mainly to correct emotional factors. Since then we have learned that this correction will balance and heal physical and mental ailments.

Root:	*Red*	*Watermelon*
2nd:	*Orange*	*Orange fruit*
Solar Plexus	*Yellow*	*Lemons (not bananas)*
Heart	*Green*	*Kiwi or green grapes*
Throat	*Blue*	*Blueberries*
3rd Eye	*Indigo*	*Plums*
Crown	*White*	*White Ice*

This information was given to me without any dialogue or explanation. No explanation is necessary when you learn about the Chakra system and the importance of colors for opening and balancing each chakra. Using foods becomes logical. Gabriel Cousens, in *Spiritual Nutrition and the Rainbow Diet* talks about this approach. He also includes complete lists of food for balancing the chakra system.

One of the most important foods that they should eat is corn and grain. If they return to the foods that the natives ate, blending it with the Ayurveda, it will help the impact of the cultures. Fruits from the native trees. Food they can grow should be the message that you aim for. If it can't be grown then they should not eat it.

Corn and Grain are both gold/white foods. This will help to open the crown chakra as well as being good for the body. In addition to changing the food we eat, we should take the maxim, "If you can't grow it, then don't eat it!"

If the world had to give up all food and have only one besides water, it would be fruit. Fruit is the one food that with variety will give all the nutrients you *need. It is also the food that can come from other regions and when eaten by itself will not upset your balance. The slowness of aligning comes when it is competing with a **range** of food from different areas. Add Flower essences and the body doesn't know what has priority. You act as thought you like/want/need foods because you feel it is necessary to go along with everyone else — including your scientists who tell you what to do. They are worse than your religious and political leaders. If everyone would not tell others what to do and let people live and eat according to what is right for them at that time, then your people would be healthier and be able to withstand the pollutants and disease.*

When people read this passage quickly, they may feel it is contradictory to earlier information. This is not so. When we discussed using and making essences, we were talking about using essences as the **prime** source of nutrients. Here they are talking about the competition between the nutrients in food and essences. Again, to achieve the transition to a higher dimension, consume only what you need and only as much as you think is best. Listen to your body and everyone else.

Coasting is one of the best ways to rebalance yourself. Make no decisions for one week. When it comes to eating, take the first thing that comes into your hand. Don't worry about the body being out of balance re nutrients. It can survive a week with no problem When it comes to fluid, it is important the each person consumes at least one glass/hour of pure water, especially during this time.

Wiggle your toes in the sand or dirt and reconnect with your planet. People are not connected and as a result feel very unhappy and disjointed. We have just given you some simple tricks.

Eat whatever you put your hands on without a decision.

Make no decisions about other factors in your life.

Drink a glass/hour.

Wriggle your toes in sand or dirt. daily during this time.

*A person can easily return to balance with this simple remedy. It is more effective than a **fast** as your leaders are so prone to preach. Of course, it is more fun when you are with people but it is more effective if you are alone to ponder emotions and feelings that result. Each person has a different thought about the diet and about the dirt through their toes. Many will awaken the emotions of their childhood. On other planets they do this regularly. Many of your ancient people did the same. They were connected with the earth.*

You can also get food through the earth and through your skin. People should massage themselves more often with oil/water that has herbs blended. Water is less likely to absorb the herbs and it will take longer to go into the skin. You humans are so impatient! You are willing to put a scent into an oil and use it but you won't put herbs into the oil and use it the same way. You wear color and expect it to balance your emotions [which it will] *but you won't do it with herbs. Why not?*

If you do this 3 times a year, you will bring your body back into balance. Combine this with meditation and see what happens.

It is important that people focus the amount of liquid intake according to the region they live. This is not only fluid but foods. Grain is dry and appropriate for arid land. You are told to drink lots of water. But not always so. In a wet lush climate fruits are full of liquid so no need for water. The body adapts to where it is. As you move from one climate to another, yes, you need to adjust but body will balance, given the time. When you drink more than you need, it throws the body out of balance. The body needs only as much as the climate gives and needs. This is the reason for societies to become imbalance. North America is very active and busy, too much fluid. It you look at the bodies and your skin, you will see moisture given to you, as much as you need. When you live in a dry region, your skin dries out to match nature. Beauty changes to where you are. There is no need to store lots up [fluids]. *In Hot climates, many people store fluids for fear of running out — hence fat people.*

If you feel confused, listen to your body,. If you keep getting thirsty, then you should be drinking more liquid. When traveling, it is important to consume liquid, preferably from the departure place. This involves carrying bottle water. The Ayurveda doctors understood this and combined it in their diets and lifestyle recommendations.

When they eat grains and fluid, they swell up. Grain alone will not make you fat. In a moist climate, dried foods are not good. They are cold and will absorb fluid needs to keep warm. Grains and fluid will mix to help balance energy.

*How long does it take to get in tune with a regions? When you are already balanced, it doesn't take long. Most people are not concerned with **staying** balanced, they trick themselves into 'minor treats'. However minor treats add up.*

Meat is fluid. Whether you live in a dry or moist climate, include what meat you eat in total fluid intake.

This passage includes several points to remember:

1. In a moist climate, focus on fruits.

2. In a cold climate, grains are good because you need the fluid to light your internal fire.

3. Treats are OK when your body is balanced. When you think you need a food, this is more likely to be craving. Our body has a strange way of asking for foods we shouldn't eat when it is not at peace.

It is important that people consume sufficient liquid. All regions of your world can include citrus drops in their water. Even though we have talked about consuming produce from your region, citrus is one fruit that will travel and when you place it in the air of the region for at least one day, the energy will align to the region. This is because of the amount of liquid in citrus fruit. It is a way of calming and balancing the energy of the individual. It is also a way of consuming yellow. Last time we talked to you about how important yellow is for serenity. By consuming yellow fruit, it is another way. Also yellow vegetables are good but not as good as green produce. When someone is feeling unsettled, yellow fruit or citrus, it has a remarkable calming and balancing effect on the individual. Calm and yet energized. This is the feeling that all the people on your planet can achieve if they incorporate yellow fruit and clothing into their life.

Interesting that again they talk about consuming more liquid but this time they combine it with the color yellow. Yellow is the color for the third chakra. It is also a color for connection to the universe — crown chakra. This is why it is so calm. An open third chakra energizes and an open crown chakra calms.

Cactus has a good juice that is ideal for those living in a desert area. Juicing every morning is one way to get fruit and liquid for each day. Canned or frozen is a way to start.

A local area sustains those who live there. All areas have similar 'good' juice. Another area and its 'juice' would be the maple syrup from the Northeastern parts of North America. It is not a "juice" as we think of it but it provides nutrients and energy from the local nature.

It is important the people do not get over confident with taking flower essences to solve their problems and trying to balancing their body. They must learn to recognize that an imbalance is there as a signal and that they should look at their entire life and discover what is causing the imbalance. Taking essences to cope is only a temporary measure and is great for getting back into balance. But once there, they should not depend on the essences. It is like depending on your drugs that will only cause more problems. Many of your diseases that are in your world today are caused by becoming too dependent on one system. Balancing the energy is the only and best way. Ayurveda and Chinese Medicine are the two most important systems Also, it is important that you look at the indigenous people of your region to see how they ate.

Essences are included in this Food section because they are excellent for balancing and matching the energy of the Earth. If we lived in a perfect world, they would also give us all the nutrition we required to survive. Unfortunately, in the human push for 'improvement', we have taken the nutrients out of the food, flowers and plants.

There is a continuous debate about not needing supplements because our food has everything we need. Unfortunately, here too, the new hybrid plants are lacking some of the food factors. When we make essences from hybrid plants, we will not get the complete set of properties. We will, however, match the energy of our local Earth. Some of the problems facing the population today, such as schizophrenia and bi-polar are the result of nutrients being left out of our hybrid plants. Essences is a simple way of rebalancing the energy and are non-addictive. There is a great deal of research on this therapeutic method.

People who suffer from the climate of the season, do so, usually because they are eating foods that are not common to their climate and/or season. If they tried to change their diet concentrating on the foods that are appropriate, they will probably find that their depression would decrease.

The perceived invincibility of the human being causes the Season Depression (SAD) as well as many other illness. People must realize that they live in a region designed to accommodate humans in a certain manner and they should cooperate. When they do, only wellness will follow. Researching the indigenous nations and follow their pattern, will reduce some of the suffering by humans who live in a region but eat like they were somewhere else.

When it is combined with heat, or hot winds, humans should be very careful to consume the right foods and the right amount of fluids. Because people do not like to prepare food in the hot weather, they eat the wrong things. Fruit is best as well as juices. A person in the heat can live on fruit juices alone and not suffer any bad effects. The most important ones to consume are local, berries, apples, peaches, etc. The tropical juices are for those in the tropics. The punch you make should be made of local juices and minimal ice. People will wonder but it is a way for you to influence their consumption. Ginger ale, cranberry juice, peach/apricot juice and maybe apple juice. There should not be any citrus involved. Try today to mix some and see how they taste. With the number of illness affecting your people, help people become aware of what is potentially bad. Consume little meat.

This pertains to hot weather as well as the winds. Prior to this passage, the guides were talking about the direction clouds blow. Caution should be utilized when winds are blowing in a direction contrary to their usual pattern. Fruit and juice will help return the body and spirit to equilibrium. I refer you to the Environment section.

Hello. We need to remind you again of the importance of water. Unless human beings absorb enough water, or when the time comes, go to planets where there is water, they will always suffer balancing problems. As you have learned, consuming water and foods that are local, the body can stay in balance. You have picked up on the reason for jet lag being the imbalance of foods. It is now time for you to understand that jet lag and the problems that affect your bodies will be with you for many years to come. As you have discovered, the body can be a light body with no insides. There is therefore nothing to get out of balance. Once people discover that they can become a spark of light and travel as you do from place to place, there will be no jet lag. Planes will still be a way of life but the people will realize that they can put themselves in a sort of stasis and **consume only water while they travel***. Then, if they follow the regime of local foods from home and local foods from the new location, there will be no jet lag and little discomfort.*

This passage talks about the future of humans as we evolve. If you are not interested in this concept, ignore it. The remainder of the passage is important for **all,** especially those who do a lot of flying. Once we understand that we can reduce jet lag and flight discomfort simply through food and liquids, we will enjoy flying even more than we do now. Liquid is easier to balance when it is from a different region. Of course, we are talking about distilled/pure water.

Procedures such as biofeedback are effective in slowing our bodily functions. Putting us in a near stasis state, we slow our functions and reduce the requirement for nutrients. Jet lag works only when we travel in one direction. However, it is important that we follow these simple procedures traveling either way.

Grapefruit *is one of the most powerful aromas and foods. It is calming and also tells spirit that you are ready to talk. Try having it around you when you meditate and see what comes forth. Sprinkle the aroma on your stones and see what happens.*

To understand the power of grapefruit, the following is quoted from a book by Gurudas.

> ... it had the potential for pulsation of sunlight energy as people might handle or be near it. ...It strengthened the physical body and many aspects of regrowth that made it easier for sunlight energy to be transferred to people. This is ultimately to provide for mankind a greater sense of purpose and strength and a way by which the plant

kingdom can share a certain inner peacefulness and resourcefulness with mankind.

It primarily adjusts and aligns the cranial plates, which relieves pressure from the atlas. It has a regenerative effect on the body manifesting in clearer thoughts and a remedy for tension stored in the temples, head, and jaw bone. It acts as a mild tonic to the meridians and the pineal gland is stimulated.

Stress in the muscles often comes from the mental body and its association with the muscular system. An aggravated mental body often creates muscular tension. Grapefruit has, a mild direct affect on the mental body. The mental body is aligned with the rest of the system. ...When used externally, it helps absorb calcium and vitamin E. On the cellular level, protein assimilation is enhanced.

Better communication between dolphins and humans will also be noted if humans use this essence in communicating with dolphins. The vibrational rate of thought that creates a resonance between humans and dolphins is enhanced. Any negative aspects to Mercury are relieved, and the sixth ray is strengthened. [3]

It is difficult to get ill when your system is working in complete synchronicity. Minor blips can be balanced or corrected quickly with little effort. Should

---

[3] Gurudas, *Flower Essences and Vibrational Healing*, Cassandra Press, San Rafael, Ca, 1989

*more effort be needed, then **herbs** that balance the system should be used. There are sufficient herbs for each imbalance that it is easy to select herbs or remedies that grow in your area.*

Proper diet, exercise and mediation are the tools for correcting and balancing. Herbs can be used in various methods:

Essences: The energy of the plant is transferred to pure water and a few drops are taken internally, below the tongue. Most of the essences are produced using only the flower. However, it has been discovered that the energy can also be transferred from root systems and branches. The transfer process is the same.

Pill or Capsule: This utilizes all properties of the plant. It will transfer not only the energy but the nutritional properties. This method is more complete (provided they come from your local area) but does take longer than using essences.

Herb massage: It is often forgotten that nutrients can be transferred through the skin. A massage is relaxing so the herb enters the body in a non-stress atmosphere for the spirit and mind. The body will therefore, absorb the ingredients more quickly.

This book was in its final stages when I was given the following information about **Bi-Polar** disorder. After reading other parts of this book, I am sure you will agree that the solution is feasible.

I do want to stress, however, **do not follow the procedure without consultation with your health**

practitioner. It is extremely important that your body is monitored by a professional the entire time.

Postpartum and bi-polar depression are two illnesses that are very closely connected. Western medicine treat both individually with medication. The results include many side effects and even more severe mood swings. The following is what I have been told as a cure. It is more than just a remedy because that suggests that it, the illness, will come back again.

It is most important to cleanse the body of ***all*** *chemicals and toxins. The only way to do this is to go on a **complete,** controlled fast. When we say controlled, it is because there are many unpleasant reactions that the body, mind and spirit will display. The control is one of science to make sure that the body does not hurt itself.*

When we say it involves the body, mind and spirit it is because a) the body has been subjected to many chemicals and foods that it cannot handle. b) The mind because of the pleasure it receives from the chemicals and the pollution it has received. Bodily pollution affects the mind as well. c) The spirit because our spirit is torn between wanting serenity and wanting the horror. It almost like being possessed, as you call, it by the devil and good. We, all spirits, have a side of us that craves the evil as well as the good. Most souls have dealt with the evil in our lives. There are many on your planet that suffer from this dichotomy. Your society has many jokes about the good and bad angels on your shoulders.

*The fast should last at least 12 days and consist of **only** pure water. Water from the center of the Earth. When it is time to break the fast, do so with pure juices, no citric. The juice, should be from your region . Continue this for four days. Gradually include fruits and then slowly expand the diet. Record all the foods and the reactions. There is usually several foods that cause a reaction. They should be avoided from now on as they bring about the imbalance within the body. When you are dealing with an imbalance such as this, we do not say that you can have them occasionally. This does not allow for weakness.*

*The place of the fast should be serene, near water and forests and of course, in your own area of living. The person will usually find that they cannot tolerate meat. This is not an allergy but rather an intolerance. An intolerance can be waved occasionally. It is the chemicals that **cannot** be tolerated.*

This remedy/solution works for both men and woman who suffer from bipolar. You all have hormones. Good luck.

At this point, you may be asking "How can I apply this to my life?"

- Search out markets that sell local and organic produce.

- Review the chapter, making a list of those foods you eat and the page number.

- Select a maximum of *two* foods a week to introduce into your diet.

- Tell one person what you are doing. (this keeps you honest!)

Read on to discover some of the benefits of sensory stimuli and be prepared to make note of these.

Sensory Stimuli and the Importance of Using *All* Our Senses

There are many windows for balance within our bodies and with our environment. Some of them, like food, are internal. Others, like colors stimulate our senses and organs from without. These are some of the simplest ways to bring balance into our lives. We tend to forget that *any* vibration aligns our energy within our being. All our senses, seeing, hearing, smelling, tasting and feeling give us vibrational information. Just because we cannot see it with the naked eye does not mean that the vibration does not exist. When we align the vibration, we are able to move along the Inner Bridges, connecting all parts of our bodies with each other and with the environment surrounding us. Any stimuli will open the connection with our emotions and can be used to understand who we are and what is around us.

We, as residents of the Earth Plane, were given the blessing, or curse according to your perspective, of five senses. As we move to the fifth dimension, we will use our telepathic sense, thereby expanding these senses to six. We need to become aware of the influence of the environment and sensitivity of our senses to our harmony. We are discovering that the senses, when out of balance, can affect the magnetism and balance of our bodies, our concentration (brain) and our connection to the universe (soul).

When first inhabiting the Earth Plane, there was only the sounds of your trees and animals. According to your folklore, you left the Garden of Eden and became corrupt and polluted with the need for entertainment beyond what nature provided. This over the years has done great damage to your senses. Lately, the pollution has become even greater. Humans, in their desire for more money, possessions and greatness started producing equipment that would help them. This is not unlike robots that get out of control. This equipment provided a blanket to the sensitivity of your senses. No longer were you able to hear the slightest movement in the forest. No longer could you smell the sweetness of grass and leaves. No longer could you taste the subtitles of your food. You demanded heavier spices. No longer could you see the variety of colors. Languages of the indigenous peoples of many lands have many, many words to describe what the modern languages use only one. Your hands and feet are kept covered so that you have lost the sensitivity of touch. You cannot feel the different between leaves or between the skin of two humans. Some of this will come back with training but some is lost. As you move into the fourth dimension, you will use the telepathy to detect differences and this will enable you to communicate with others in the universe. There is no reason why you, as humans cannot use modern technology and still have the benefit of the senses that were given to you.

Piano *The top five notes on a piano are not a good vibration for your bodies. You are better to focus* *on the lower notes and octaves. This applies to people in your region. If people are in a different region, they maybe able to tolerate the higher notes. Again if a person was born elsewhere and spent most of their life in different regions. Test the notes and see how your body reacts.*

These notes are everywhere in your life. It is not just music. They may come from cars, furnaces, machinery, talking voices. Familiarize yourself with the sound and see where they occur in your world. A tuning fork is another good way to find out what notes are best for you. Also as your DNA changes, these notes will also change. Check this about every three months and note the change.

Eyes*.When we look at something bright, it throws our body into an imbalance, forcing us to realign. Similarly dark rooms will throw us into an imbalance the other way. It is important to keep rooms light but not too bright and the times in nature, avoid the bright light. This is why arid/hot climates are sources for trouble. The energy is thrown into an imbalance by the bright light. Dark northern climates are more apathetic. They usually don't care about what is going on. The ideal is a bright day, not too much sun, or stay in the shade. This is another reason for the depression that occurs when it is cloudy. When this happens, it is best to consume foods that balance the energy in the body. People go for the wrong solution because they have been listening to scientists who are not aware of the energy system of the body.*

The Ayurvedic and Chinese health systems takes changes in climate into their teachings. Look at when there is a need to change or alter the intake and exercise of the body.

Colors are a gift that the universe has given those living on Earth. You may have heard stories or tales of other planets being gray and dull and no emotions. Earth was given the colors to help match emotions. It is one of the lessons that humans must learn is how to control the emotions that are woken up by the colors around. You have the emotions that many feel put you at a lower evolution level. This is not necessarily so. Emotions make you feel alive but it is also a tool that is used to teach compassion and caring. You can surround yourself with any color you wish. However, the colors will put you into emotions that you may not want. Until you learn to manage your emotions, take the time to pay attention to the colors around you. This is not only the colors you wear. It is the colors in your buildings and the colors in nature. You humans need so much balancing and peace and yet it is so simple.

Colors also vibrate at different rates so that until you learn to "hear" the colors, you must rely on your eyes.

*Ask someone who is blind what they feel when they hold different colors and you will understand. When all of the universe has learned to manage emotions with colors, **then** other planets will begin to have color on them. You may remember when we talked about your home planet and the walled garden that only a few were allowed to enter. This is because only a few* *were allowed to or had learned to manage their emotions. Your garden of Eden was so full of color but it was not managed. It was abused. It saddened us to see this abuse. Your planet has so much to offer.*

It is important that humans remember that it is a training or learning ground for other beings and the one lesson is to manage emotions through the use of color. First humans must learn to recognize colors and the role they play.

This information came through as I was starting to compile the section on color. They felt that enough had not been said. We, as humans have the gift of color all around us and yet, we abuse it. We are encouraged to believe that color is at the whim of fashion designers. Parks, full of color, are for when we have time. We tend to forget that color and all that surrounds us affects us and can be used as a healing remedy as well as a step toward our Garden of Eden that many feel was taken from us. In reality, it was not taken but our senses were altered so that we would not recognize it.

Green *is a slow energy. Any fruit or vegetable that is green is slower and will help to balance the earth energy around you....this means that when you live in a lush forest, the energy is already slow. You may need to eat green to balance or you may need red or yellow...white is neutral. When there are red sunsets, it is an indication that you need more green to calm down the red. This is contrary to what people think. They think of red sunsets as very peaceful. They are but the scenery will leave you more alive and tuned* *into the surroundings. The energy you are around or consume will help you become more in balance with the surround energy. Green being slower means that it takes the energy of the nature to help put you in tune with the energy of your surroundings.*

It is interesting to observe that green is slow and is also related to the heart chakra, which is our connection with the world and those around us. It is a peaceful energy.

This piece of channeling refers to red and yellow. These are the lower chakra colors, connected to emotion and survival. If you are familiar with the chakras, then you will understand that we need to have all chakras of equal intensity and vibration for balance and peace in the body. It is then that we will enjoy the emotions we have been given. They will not control our actions but rather, we will be able to use emotions as they are intended; to share love and energy with others when it is needed.

If you have a garden around your home, it is important that you plant it to compliment and blend with the environment around it. For example, in a rain forest, plant rain forest plants. It is also important that should you want to have agitating colors, such as a red rose, that you have more of calm around to make it balanced. A rose garden is not calming and serene because the flowers are more active. They should be placed in a garden that will balance it and keep it calm.

Spiders are the most misunderstood of your world. They are busy but they also know how to relax and be in the now. When they weave a web, most of you think it is to catch food. That is only part of the reason. They are there to rest, enjoy the nature around them and to socialize. They can walk from one web to the next. If you hear the silence, then you can hear a sound. Because they are small, they are ignored. Their sound is one of the most beautiful, peaceful sounds. A few people have tried to copy it without knowing but they were unsuccessful. Brahms is one of the closest. Their color is also ignored. They have the widest range of colors but most people are not aware because they do not take the time, nor are your eyes sensitive enough to identify the colors. They look black to most of you and yet, black has so many ranges of color that it is delight to view. Black with a green will allow the spider to hide. The webs have all the colors and the spider can pick the main color to allow it to hide if it wants to.

This is an example of combining our awareness with the importance of color. We can learn how to hide or become invisible by adopting the colors of where we are. Increasing our knowledge will also teach us to wear black and white with a key color as the focal point. I am referring to the creating of the color. When black or white is made, we can ask for more of one color that another. When I think of this, I think of crows or starlings birds. Both are black and yet they look very different when we take the time to study them. This also goes for swans and other white birds.

Yellow *is a color right now that is important. Yes, it indicates power and intellect, but it is important that* *people use their personal power and intellect to put a stop to what they do not like. Each person can start small on their own personal world and this in turn will expand into a bigger circle, like an eddy. Yellow will give confidence that people can stand up for what they believe and do it with love of the human race and all other races on your planet and beyond.*

Most people will not blend yellow and pink or green and yet this is a combination that gives the power and strength as well as the love and healing that is required.

For you, you already know how to stand up for what you believe, you need the quiet confidence that will pass on to other people. **Blue, green and indigo are for you.** *The amethyst is your best stone. Take the time to 'fly' around the world shedding your love and power to those who need it. It is like sprinkling stardust over everyone while they sleep.*

This was a personal message for myself. However, it applies to many in our world. Once a person has gained the confidence of yellow, then they can transfer this confidence over to another color to gain what is needed at the next stage of growth. Again, I refer to the chakras. The root chakra is red and is needed for survival. As we move up the body, the colors soften and indicate a quiet confidence and connection with the universe around us.

Yellow is a color that is not being used in your world very much. It is a color that can brighten the spirits or mind and yet is tranquil and calm. It is a good color for you. When you purchase clothing, be selective and chose only colors that will bring more into your life. Yellow is calm and yet brings happiness. It is interesting that in the Joseph story with the coat of many colors, it was the multiple colors that caused his brothers to create evil. Had the coat been only yellow or soft high vibrations, he would not have been harmed.

Yellow is a color that brings balance into our spirit. Most of us think of aggression when we think of violence or hostility. This is **red**. Most think of blues, indigos and purples when we think of tranquility and calmness. Yellow gives us the strength, quiet aggression, to stand up for what is right and good. Yet, it also gives us the tranquility of a cheerful outlook.

Even though we have talked about consuming produce from your region, citrus is one fruit that will travel and when you place it in the air of the region for at least one day, the energy will align to the region. This is because of the amount of liquid in citrus fruit. It is a way of calming and balancing the energy of the individual. It is also a way of consuming yellow. Last time we talked to you about how important yellow is for serenity. Consuming yellow fruit, it is another way. Also yellow vegetables are good but not as good as green produce. When someone is feeling unsettled, eating yellow fruit or citrus, has a remarkable calming and balancing effect on the individual.

The section on **food** talks in detail about foods and how they impact our lives. The emphasis here is, not on the food, but the color of food. We are being shown that there are many ways to incorporate something into our beings.

Yellow is also the color of some of the outer planets. While a traveler may look at them and see only gray, the true color or essence is yellow. Your home planet is yellow. Do you remember how calm you feel when you come home. Calm and yet energized. This is the feeling that all the people on your Earth Plane can achieve if they incorporate yellow fruit and clothing into their life.

Yesterday, the green of the leaves came through as important. Today, orange was present and this I took into a meditation.

*Orange is the color of emotion chakra and green the heart, color of love and healing. We need to bring our emotions and love together for the peace and preservation of our planet. All colors are important and are all part of **One**, whether it is white or black. We need to display all colors but these two are all important. Remember when orange was so important in the late 60s and early 70s. This was when people were starting to acknowledge their emotions and right to be. Many people consider Aquarius as the catalyst but orange had a part also.*

Both orange and green are the softer sides of yellow, the intellectual analysis. We need to encourage people to water down their intellectual/analytical side of themselves.

I have found that there are many times when I was channeling that the same thing was being said but in a different manner. When something was important, like humans, my spirit guides repeat a message several times to make sure we get it. I encourage you to take time to review history and note what colors were prevalent at various times.

What color is the wind? Does it matter? The wind is an invisible friend that is with you at all times. Yellow shows that it is alive, vibrant and cheerful. Red becomes assertive and cleansing. Blue is calming and gentle. Green is healing. It cleanses the air coming into your lungs. We fly on all colors and do not care about color. However, it is useful to have a color when you are prescribing to people. If the standard is accepted, then they know that they need a certain color. It is important to remember that invisible, black and white includes all colors. When you need a certain color, you will see the color in different things around you. You may, for example, all of a sudden, notice the color of birds, cars, flowers. When you continually see a specific color, put that color into the wind and check out your feelings. You will see certain colors linked with different parts of the world, the wind will carry that color.

Most of us do not think of wind as having a color. We do know that colors have a vibration. Wind vibrates. In time, we will be learn to listen to all around us and know the wind's vibration. Once we know this, we will be able to translate this into a color.

Do you notice how many people are receptive about aligning the energy. It has been said for many years. People have read it but never talked about.

Now when you refer to it, or talk about it, they agree and open up

Yellow *is particularly good for people with heart problems, communication.*

Blue *is good for blood issues.*

Green *is good for anybody who lives in an apartment and is not in nature. It is also good for arthritis.*

Red *is good for foot problems*

Purple *for back.*

Orange *for skin conditions.*

Blue-purple *is good for hair problems, whether it be a hair loss or too much such as female hair on face.*

They can use or carry a stone, wear a piece of clothing or carry a small piece of cloth. This should be done for not less that two months. At home, candles of these colors will help. When you work with sick people, give gifts of colored candles and other items in the appropriate color.

Colors can be used by the health provider, the caregiver or the individual themselves. A caregiver can have blankets of various colors and simply use the best one for each person.

Certain essences are associated with certain sickness labels. Learn them... You can ask people to hold a certain color when checking them for essences.

The essences referred to are the Pacific Flower Essences that I use as a healing remedy. This technique combines the healing of color with the healing of an essence. Essences have been shown to alter the vibration of the internal body faster than color alone.

February is normally a time for people to get depressed. However, it is an opportunity for joy. This is a time when you can clean out old skeletons and get ready for the new, lively energy that is soon to be upon you. For some who live in warm climates, this is a birth time. Enjoy whatever time you are in for each time will give you an opportunity to discover something new, whether it is about yourself or about nature or others around you. You should always be looking for new opportunities to learn and remember and tell others that learning is the best part of living there is. This doesn't matter whether you are on the Earth Plane or another plane. Even advanced beings and cultures are learning. They will learn at a calmer level. When you saw yourself as a light being, this light being was learning. It had to learn how to move amongst the trees on your Earth. It had to learn how to reach new stars. There are always some planets that are not receptive. Some planets give off a high heat and energy. A light being landing on them, or if you touched them, will discover the heat to be too intense. It is almost like becoming burned. This is when knowing colors is useful. When you look at the natural colors of nature, you can discover which are the hottest. This does not always match what you think of when you see colors.

Yellow *is a hot color. It will burn should you light on it.*

Red *is energizing but is cooling to touch.*

***Green** is the safest color on **any** planet. It is cool and calming. Even your home planet has lots of green and it is the color that feeds **all** species, even your bees.*

***Blue** is not a color to touch. It is stinging and is present only to look at. It shows up all the other colors so they can be appreciated.*

***Purple** is safe only for those who have energized and balanced their bodies. Young children should be kept away from this color on a general basis. Of course, there are some children who arrive already vibrating at a higher level and **know** what is safe.*

***Orange** is a toxin. When you touch orange on a steady basis, you will feel agitated and uncomfortable.*

This does not apply to what you wear or what you surround yourself. These are colors that will enhance your vibration and allow you to evolve faster and higher. Many of your people are not interested in evolution and they should stay with soft colors. The strong colors will cause or aggravate dis-ease and disorders in their body.

The time they refer to as birth time is Spring, Summer as growing and Winter as death or sleeping time. The last sentence refers to soft and strong colors. This is looking more at the **tone,** or intensity of the color.

Life is gentle. A breeze should never become a storm. Most of you spend so much time and energy trying to change the ways things are. Have you ever noticed how the colors in nature are so diverse and yet so gentle. Your part of the world is meant to have soft colors. They should be incorporated into your life. The only time you will see stronger colors is before it gets cold. Then the bold colors will attract beings to it so that they can store food for the long cold times. This is the same as life itself. Life should not have storms. Look for the soft colors and events. They will do more for you than if you go for loud music, busy activities or argumentative people who are trying to change the way things should be.

*Yes, you come into life to learn certain lessons but **all** lessons can be learned without going after bold colors or angry people. Part of the lessons you are meant to learn is **how** to achieve the goals in a gentle manner. Whenever you get frustrated or angry ... **stop** ... and ask "How can I achieve the same end without being bold, angry, busy, noisy?" I am willing to bet that with thought you will find an answer.*

Other parts of the world do have bold colors and more anger. These are people who are younger and have many lessons to learn before they are allowed to come back into the more gentle regions. Do you find it interesting that the oldest records of people is in the warmer climates? Yet the records of other worlds is in the colder or higher climates. This should tell you something. The hot climates are to introduce people to your world. The other climates are for wiser, more evolved people. This is why there are so many wars in the hot climates. They also, naturally have bold colors.

Peace will come through gentle colors, gentle life and not trying to change nature but honoring and loving it the way it comes. Deserts are beautiful if only people would take the time to enjoy. Rain forests are also beautiful. Tundra and very cold regions also have a beautiful that can only be enjoyed by those who truly understand.

Go gently, my loved one.

This passage supports the passage above when they speak of yellow and the higher colors of blue, violet and indigo as being peaceful. The end of this passage is how most of the channeling ends. They are truly gentle and only want for us to be gentle, balanced, and at peace.

Blue *is one of the most important colors for you. It brings tranquility and peace. If you feel scattered as you were yesterday, stop and get something blue, hold it and then put it in your clothing. A dark blue is best. You were right with the purple you are wearing, dark is calmer for you but not everyone.*

When bringing in the colors of the chakras, bring them in through the crown and then see them parallel in the body, moving down beside one another and moving in unison, dancing. This is a way to get a feel of the energy and what it should look like wherever you live, desert or forest.

A blue dish, flowers and herbs. You are being passed a great gift. Use it wisely. Good luck. Spend much time in the garden. Being with the soil will be very balancing for you. Hummingbirds will be prevalent at this time.

Prior to including this in the text, there has been a large discussion about yellow, suggesting that this was the only optimum color. All colors are good and we should remember the importance of each one.

For those who like to have pets, a yellow canary is good. It is yellow. Energizing and yet calming. When you take on the responsibility of a pet, you should realize that you are given the responsibility of caring for its soul. Healing and talking is important. A contract has been made with the soul of a pet and yourself. It has agreed to be a pet, confined to help you and others learn. It is the greatest gift that a soul can give. Today your pet met several small children. It was kissing one, more than the other and more than she does with many humans. It was her way of giving healing to that person and his soul. While the person will not remember, the soul will. This is the true power of healing and the true gift of love and healing.

*The **colors** you saw this morning are the colors of peace. It is important that they be worn on your body. Blue, green and red. Your mountains were talking to you as was the seal. Next time, stop and listen.*

*Hello. You have been asking about the connection between hawks and swans. All birds and species are connected with each other. We tend to forget that all have a dual set of attributes. The hawk is a hunter and can be ruthless but it is also an excellent mother and cares for offspring. It will warn those around it of danger. So is the same for the swan. It is known for its grace but it can also be ruthless at hunting. You tend to look at **white** as beauty. Is not gray and other colors beautiful? The love of **white** as beauty has* *come from your cultures. We talked this week about how much learning comes from your parents and is programming. So it is with color. Right now you are being taught to avoid red and yellow. Why? Red is one of the most beautiful colors. It is alive but there is also a serenity and peace attached to it. Every time that you judge, look for the opposite and you will see that the other side should or could be the side that is important. Again we come back to balance. When you paint, try using opposite **colors** and see what effects you can get. Will it bring a feeling of balance to the viewer? You will find it often does. Look at the tones and hues when choosing opposites. Again, we say, bring into your diet all elements, top of trees and roots of plants. This is balance. The same balance as the colors and wildlife bring to you. People need to realize that the balance is the most important thing in life. Your food philosophy called macrobiotics is all about balance. They are concerned about balancing the yin/yang. Chinese medicine is about balance. So is Ayurveda. Balance work and play. Balance soft and loud music. **Everything in life must** be balanced. This is also the same with the elements.*

When you are in balance, you will find a peace and beauty that most have never seen before.

*Yes you can wear **yellow and red** at the same time. They are balanced on the spectrum and bring harmony into the life of the wearer and the observer.*

This may appear as a strange passage to include in the Sensory Stimuli section. However, when this is read in its entirety, you can see the importance of color throughout the writing. Color is only one tool for observation.

Blankets. *Many of your people think blankets are unimportant in your spiritual growth but we ask you to look at the colors of what you sleep under. When we lived on your earth, our colors were very bright and alive. This was because we could handle, and in fact, needed the energy to keep up alive in your system. For you, you are better to have a calm color and yet still allow us, invite us, to come to visit.*

Try an experiment. Select two blankets. For one week sleep under one and observe the energy and spiritual activity the following day. Then rest with a neutral color for one week. Next, for one week also, choose a color that is the opposite of the first color you choose. Again, note how you felt and what went on in spiritual and physical activity. Each one of you is different and require different energies. Again, the region will have an impact. If you live in a darker, cooler and wetter climate, the brighter colors will make you feel alive and the darker will be restful. When someone lives in the tropics, a brighter, vibrant color can be very disturbing. The people in these climates do wear bright colors but for sleeping and resting, it is important that they make the change to a more restful tone.

It has been acknowledged that a great deal of healing and communication occurs in the dreamstate while sleeping. When this sleep is surrounded with a vibrant, energizing color, the healing and communication can become erratic. Sometimes though, we recognize the need for the vibrancy for healing and balancing. Strong colors can speed up healing and invite deeper communication with our souls, our past and our spirit guides. Being in balance will allow us to discriminate times for peaceful balancing and enthusiastic communication. Like everything else in our lives, we need both ends of the continuum and all ranges in between.

Hello. **Aromas** *are one of the easiest paths to connecting all your senses. So many of your people consider aromas as being completely separate from the other senses, but we ask you. When you see color in nature, do you not get a sense of smell. Almost everyone could give a smell that is connected to color. Sounds have a smell. Most do not think of this connection because you have been taught to separate all your senses. As you evolved, you spent time analyzing and not feeling. We have often said that you are blessed (and cursed) with emotion. For those who have live on planets that do not have emotion, we turned instead to aromas to give pleasure. Even a dark, damp planet has aromas. The beings who come from there can tell the difference between many smells. People who live with color around them can pick out subtle differences of color. It is the same with aromas. All your senses are very accurate but through time you have been taught to ignore and look instead at other aspects. A rose is considered beautiful if it is large, few on a stem and the color is pretty to look at. Through time, the colors are given a higher priority than the aroma. Yet, it is the aroma that brings peace of mind,* *reminding us of memories from our past. It will even remind you of other lives without understanding where the smell comes from.*

We started out by saying that aromas connect all the other senses when trying to balance your body.

Aromas have tones or notes. Color has tones or notes. Touch has tones or notes. Touch has a smell that is often used.

When you look at nature, how often do you touch something and then smell your hand or the object to see if it is fresh, safe, friendly. All creatures use the sense of smell to identify other creatures. There is also a tone or note attached to this. As anger increases, the smell will change to a dark, heavy one.

To bring the body into balance with the mind and spirit, we recommend practicing and relearning your senses. It will take time but you should be able to do this with practice.

First. We recommend working with someone else who can provide you with a range of smells without you looking. Rather than concentrating on trying to identify each one, ask these questions.

- *Is it heavy?*
- *Is it fresh?*
- *What color would you give it?*
- *What does it feel like (touch)?*
- *What emotion do you get?*

All these questions should be asked and answered with your sense of smell. You may get frustrated but it will come.

Once you have improved your sense of smell, go out into nature and look at the trees, grass, rocks. What smells do you get? Can you answer the questions the same as before. There will be no right answer. It is very personal and will be a reference for you.

This same exercise can be followed with feeling with your hands.

The same with taste. Because there are objects that can be poison, take a small piece into your mouth mixed with water, swish it around your mouth and spit it out. This way you will not take poisons into your body. You will be using only a small portion of your taste abilities but these are the safest.

Again, when you are improving you can try to swallow tastes that you are confident are not poison. Ask the same questions.

As you practice with your sense of smell, seeing, tasting and feeling you can then look at your hearing. Many blind people on your planet have developed strong hearing ability. In your world there is so much noise putting you into imbalance that you have learned to shut sounds out. We encourage you to open your hearing and then you will be able to close it off when you do not need it or when it is putting you into a state of imbalance.

Relearning your senses will allow you to hear and feel when we are with you from the spirit world. You will learn to adjust your mind without effort.

The result is a very peaceful entity.

This has been a practical session. Before we close, we would like to talk to you about things happening in your world.

You were asked this morning why someone is feeling a spirit who passed over 10 years ago. As your people become more in balance and receptive, you will become more aware of entities who are on the other side. This is to the credit of the Earth bound spirits. This was the situation with the young person. She should be very proud.

To stay cool in the warm weather you are experiencing, we refer you to the mustard bath that we have talked about so many times. It is not only the water that will cool you, the mustard will do it also. Again, if you think cool, you will be cool. If you think any discomfort, you will be uncomfortable. You can change whatever you want just by thinking. The scientists who have created all the drugs will not be happy to hear this because they want the population to be sick and angry so they can control. Each human being on the Earth Plane can be in control and give love without any force from others. By being in control of your body and sending love, this will create a force that will push back. Yes, there will be many who are frustrated and angry but when your people learn to stay balanced and totally connected, there will be such a force that anger cannot exist.

This passage is exciting and challenging. We **have** become complacent about our senses. We tend to use our nose to inform us about the extremes — very pleasant or extremely unpleasant and potentially dangerous. We ignore all the other information that is available to us. Unless we are, or have been, without eyesight we do not listen to all that is around us. Some meditation schools recommend that we go out into a park or other natural setting for at least one day and experience life without conversation or machinery noises. They are looking at it only from one perspective, healing and tranquility. We need to use this to help us bring our being into balance and aid communication with all aspects of our being.

In addition to the recommendations that came through the channeling, I recommend that you start with only one or two sensations. If it is possible, shut out all other sensations that our world supplies. Do not judge yourself. You may read a book that states that one smell or sensation means one thing. Yet you think something else. Then accept your interpretation. For you it is correct.

To help you get started, here are some of the accepted connections. Please remember, you are the best expert for interpretation.

Using Aroma for Balance.

Use this only when you have used food and lifestyle as the prime balancer. It is important to remember it is not an alternative to other remedies. However, it will fix small imbalances.

Aromas are useful maintaining balance when you travel over long distance. For complete connection, you still need to plan food intake before and after flights that connect with the regions involved.

Research has separated aromatic oils into base, middle and top "notes." Top notes evaporate faster (higher vibration) than a middle or base. When a perfume or oil is blended, it is important to combine oils that evaporate at different rates. Science also separates oils into feminine and masculine. What we have done instead is indicate which oils are best for balancing each of our body, mind and spirit.

Body: Earth based, feminine, calming

Mind: Masculine, clarity, astuteness and brightness

Spirit: Feminine, soft and spicy.

Apart from traveling, when you are balanced and want to enhance and maintain connection, use a blend of all three notes. There are times in our lives when we want to emphasize one more than the others. It is then appropriate to place more importance on one over the others. Remember though that too much and too often will help to throw the body off. Being attuned to your body will tell you when this happens.

The following suggested list follows the scientific guidelines:

Base Notes
For the Body (Androgynous Scents)

Cedarwood	Cinnamon	Frankincense
Heliotrope	Labdanum	Meliot
Myrrh	Oakmoss	Patchouli
Sandalwood	Vanilla	

Middle Notes
For the Body (Feminine Scents)

Cardamom	Carnation	Clary-Sage
Clove	Geranium	Ginger
Linden	Marjoram	Nutmeg
Rosemary	Rosewood	Thyme

For the Mind (Masculine Scents)

Anise	Basil	Bay
Caraway	Carrot	Coriander
Cumin	Lavender	Moss
Oregano	Sage	Tarragon

For the Mind (Feminine Scents)

Hyacinth	Jasmine	Jonquil
Mandarin	Neroli	Peppermint
Pine	Rose	Ylang-Ylang

Top Notes
For the Soul (Masculine Scents)

Mandarin	Lemongrass	Peppermint
Sage	Verbena	

For the Soul (Feminine Scents)

Angelica	Anise	Armoise
Bergamot	Chamomile	Estragon
Galbanum	Juniper	Lemon
Lime	Marigold	Orange
Petitgrain	Roman	Spearmint

For people who are just becoming interested in spirituality and personal health, they may not be interested in this information. Others will find it to be just what they were looking for. Again, I encourage all readers to incorporate what appeals to them. There is little scientific research on some of the topics such as aromatherapy. However, there are many people who are firm believers in the success. Even if you consider it a placebo, if it works for you, use it.

Sensory stimuli fits very well with the topic of our next chapter — Exercise. Exercise and fitness is one of the best connections of body, mind and spirit. You can review the stimulations discussed in this chapter and choose a color or perhaps an aroma to go with your fitness program. Your music choice will smooth your fitness path. In addition, it might even speed up the transition.

The Exercise Connection

This section is short but this does not diminish its importance. Religions around the world have combined exercise into their spiritual practices. And yet, many still do not consider exercise as an important part of integrating body, mind and spirit or as part of our evolution. Exercise that puts you in a meditative state as well as getting the body fit are the most powerful forms. This includes walking, swimming, soft martial arts, or cycling. One of our objectives is to ensure that **all** our "Inner Bridges" are crossed in equal uniformity. When we use only one tool to cross only one inner bridge, such as mind to spirit, we may throw another bridge, possibly the body to mind bridge, out of equilibrium.

Exercise also provides an opportunity, possibly the best, to combine **all** tools to ensure that each inner bridge is crossed. For example, you can carry, or wear, the colors according to what you need at that time. Eating the right balancing foods **before** going for your meditative exercise starts the balance process for your body. A meditative exercise will enhance the color purple and connect with the universal spirits. Being out in nature, brings in the color green that will open the heart. This brings the spirit and body together as well as using the time to heal minor imperfections in the health of the body. Wearing a red sweater or riding a red bicycle opens the root chakra. This is useful technique when you need to remember who you are, in both spirit, body and mind.

While there has not been a large amount of information from the spirit writers, this does not suggest we ignore this small section. It allows room for the individual's creativity. Since there have been many books written on each form of exercise, once you find a program that interests you, I suggest that you research the books and find what is right for you.

Exercise*. Exercise should be equal to the energy speed of the region you are living in. Tropical climates have the energy moving at a slower pace ... Rainforest and mountains seem to have a faster pace.*

When they talk about being equal to the region, it is important that we either keep it at a par or slow the speed according to the climate. For example, in a tropical climate, we do not want to slow it down further. Nor, do we want to speed up the rainforest to excess.

This is a situation where you can look at the types of exercise according to Ayurveda. This philosophy categories according to the energy of the region.

Swimming, only in the right climate would be good for aligning the energy ... so it is with Tai Chi, Yoga, Chi Gong. All will work to some extent in other climates but for true alignment, stay with the region you are in.

Swimming is good in climates that are warm. In a cold climate, it would throw the body out of alignment. Since the water is already too cold, swimming makes the body colder.

The exercise that we take part in is important to the alignment of our energies. We should look at the color, the brightness and also the loudness of the activity. For example. fast exercise will almost always speed up our energy. Bright, noisy ones will not calm us and will put us into an imbalance. If you are in a fast season, faster color or bright room, then it is important to use an exercise that is calming that will bring you back to the center. We should always strive to find the center of what we are doing. Running will not give us time to pick up the center of our surroundings and will leave us out of balance..We cannot pick up the energy of the wildlife when we are moving too fast.

Exercise as it is talked about does not always create a meditative condition. It is appropriate to be selective and include a variety of exercise with different objectives.

When we are in a moister climate, then we need to consider the energy we are picking up from the environment and match it to the energy of the exercise.

Walking and other mild exercises *is one of the best ways to balance and cleanse your body. This is using your skin for the purpose we gave it. It also encourages functioning of all parts of the body. Walking in silence and in tune with nature is one of the better ways as it will help the organs in your bodies align with what is around you. Walking beside water should be balanced with walking in a forest. The same* *goes for different regions. Walking in a desert should be balanced with walking in the scrub. Swimming in the ocean should be balanced with walking in the gardens.*

Bicycles. *You have created transportation called a bicycle. Note the structure. Your movie ET used a bike to reach the stars. This was in fun but in reality, the structure and principles in bikes are good. The wheels represent the life force and the number two. The gears --by managing your life-force and the balance of two, you will be able to travel to the stars. Of course, it will take some time for your people to perfect this but the principle is there. Meditate on two wheels turning as a bike does and see what happens. Do this on a regular basis. Daily is ideal but not always practical Get the wheels moving and make sure you have a crystal to balance.*

This is not exercise but it shows how we can incorporate traditional exercise into many other purposes.

Most of the information so far suggests that the individual concentrates on getting into balance by his or her self. For the most part, this is best. However, once we understand the influence of family and friends as discussed in the next section, it may be appropriate to work together. For example: If you feel balance is needed for the family unit, you may want to exercise together with a specific color or music. This will bridge the internal body, mind and spirit and will also connect the beings with each other.

Family and Social Influence

The human being is a very social animal. We need others around us and we need to be loved. When there is strife or tension within the family or when a social influence is negative, it is very important that we, as individuals, work to bring it into harmony. What can we do?

We can include others in our chosen method of balancing body, mind and spirit. Examples would be group meditations, exercise or decorating the surroundings with the right color.

We also need to recognize when a situation is **not** in our best interest and step back. When we do not take action, we tend to focus on the issue and this distracts us from our goal. As I am sure you realize that it is generally accepted that when you worry about anything, your body can get sick. It will also throw you out of balance since you spend the time thinking of what is unnecessary and avoid spending the time connecting with the spirit or maintaining a physical balance.

The following passage was channeled through someone else from an entity named ALDA in May, 2000. Alda talks about love and balance. Read on.

Look around you now. What have you got. A family of love. Sure there are certain things one or the other will say, "I don't understand why they are doing this or that way." That is what a family is all about. Each one of you, when you open and tell others what you need or how you feel, they will all come together and help you. Think of many who are not here at this time and also think that each and every one is connected with others. This family grows and each and every one learns to listen, to feel what the other, at the moment, is thinking or feeling.

When you worry, you lose energy. If you have anything going wrong with the body, worry worsens it. If anything is not working in the body, you need your energy to straighten out imbalances or take on viruses and bacteria in the body. You make them go away by not worrying and draw in the energy. By going out and touching a blade of grass, you draw the energy and touch that tree. Any tree you see. **Do not** *look at it and say "nice." Touch it and stop worrying and thinking what will happen to me. Take all your worries. Put them on your lap and look at it. Send energy to it and let go. Face it and know nothing will happen to you. You will live. Look at a mountain and think. How many years has that survived. Take it inside you. You can survive as long as you want to.*

When we realize that we are all family, and all will help one another (and they will!), we can have the love for all. Personally, I have known for many years that we should love all but I found it difficult. I thought about people who criticized me or robbed someone I knew. I found it very difficult to send love to them. Remember, even the murderer or robber needs your love. Worry and revenge keep you from sleeping, keeps you from concentration, and keeps you from staying in balance. Touching the blade of grass or touching the tree is a way of passing the worries to other parts of the Universe and letting them provide the healing.

Hello. Family is the one part of changing your lives that you tend to forget. Many souls, or rather, all souls come to the Earth for lessons. These lessons also help in the understanding of how to improve the human so there is a connection to the universe. Families are selected for you by the Total and the individual souls agree to enter a family. Because the learning includes the learning to live in a physical body, there are lessons transferred from one space in time to the next through these families. Each soul is challenged to learn through these combined barriers. We have talked a great deal about the importance of learning to balancing the body, mind and spirit so that the humans on the Earth Plane can evolve to a higher dimension. Each soul does have an age of maturation but the body is a barrier. The older the soul, the better able are they to handle, understand and move beyond the barrier of the physical. It doesn't matter how hard some souls try to move to a higher dimension, if their physical barriers are so strong sometimes they cannot be changed. This is also part of the lessons of the soul.

Let us explain in more detail. A soul comes to the Earth Plane to learn lessons that the soul needs for evolvement. On the Earth Plane, the physical body lives in time dimensions that move forward in a mass group. Millions of souls lived in what you call the middle ages. Later, these same souls moved into the next century. While on the Earth Plane in each time period, the body, or genes, remembered certain events and conditions. This is carried forward on the physical level. The soul is separate from this memory. However, the soul, to grow, must learn how to blend this knowledge into the soul knowledge. Therefore, there are two parallel paths of knowledge. One is physical, from body to body, passing through genes. The other is the soul's knowledge, taken from the Total.

In order for the soul to evolve and return to the Total, it must learn to combine both these paths of knowledge. The human on the Earth Plane is faced with a great challenge. The genetic knowledge is unfamiliar to the soul's Total knowledge and it(the soul) must learn how to use it.

Lets explain on a smaller level. Each soul comes into a family on your Earth Plane, let us say 4 souls, what you call a Mother and Father, a little girl and a little boy. Each of these four bodies have a memory of what happened hundreds of years ago. Each also has the memory of the lives they have lived in other parts of the universe. Now these four have to blend this knowledge. One of the four has knowledge from the soul's learning that enables it to change and use the Earthly genetic knowledge and possibly change it. Another soul in the family may not be able to alter the Earth knowledge because their universal experience limit them. [a younger soul] *This is often where what you call allergies come into play. One soul has learned how to heal or bypass this physical difficulty.*

This connection should not be forgotten. It is important. Should you be a soul that has not learned to bypass the physical, you will have to work that much harder to move to a higher dimension. It is one of your lessons in the life you are presently living.

Now that you understand the connection and differences between the two paths of knowledge, we hope you will understand why the influence of your family and society around you is important in maintaining the balance we are so anxious for each of you to reach. A family of different soul ages makes the absorption of knowledge more difficult. Each is working on a personal set of goals. Each feels that theirs is the most important. Each is trying to get everyone around him to move at the same speed as he is. Each will, at some level, be trying to persuade all around him to stay at one spot and cross a bridge only when one soul thinks it is important. Discrimination is what is important. To function on the Earth Plane, you have to follow the rules of society and yet you also have the rules of the universe. Therefore, when you have discordance within your personal group, you must search out humans who have energy that will balance the energy around you. You must have energy of the entire continuum around you. **Then,** *you can focus on using the other tools.*

This may sound very complicated. It is not really. Later, we will give you simple steps to follow so that you can connect all tools and use as ways to cross all the inner bridges. Bridges must also join all influences around you and be connected to the inner ones you are building. Rest now and we will talk later. Go with love.

This is an inner bridge between the knowledge carried by genes and the knowledge carried by our souls. The balance can appear to be very lopsided at some observation times. This is when it is important to have a balanced family unity to support and help us understand what is happening.

Over the past century, the family structure has changed drastically. Members of this structure are often living alone and trying to sort out the answers without the wisdom of the family knowledge. It is possible the soul will wait to understand what is coming forth, but the genetic knowledge must be understood as it appears. Today, in our Western society, people are so anxious to assimilate material wealth that they ignore the responsibility of the family. They assume because children are clothed, fed and kept away from physical harm that they are fulfilling their duty. The only aspect of the children's being that is being balanced is the physical well being. Their mind may be fed because of school and training that a parent assumes the 'right' way. The link between mind and body is being ignored.

Families are running in isolation with little support from the extended family. We do know that the souls who are coming to the Earth are older than many of the existing Earth souls. They are also remembering some of the genetic knowledge from past lives. Children are being treated AS children and being given small pieces of knowledge. However, they will know that it is incomplete and/or not accurate. Children question and are simply told to keep quiet or given a pill such as Ritalin. There is little time left for questions and answers in a family's busy lives. Where does this leave us, then?

- Children are unbalanced because they know the information they are asking for is incomplete. They know the information is not always accurate. They place stress upon themselves trying to figure it out.

- Parents are feeling frustrated and stressed because they don't know how to handle these children and there is no one to teach them.

- Families are broken apart because older and wiser adults want to help the children and may realize that the children of today and tomorrow already have the answers. These adults are ignored and cast aside by new parents.

- Children get the food for the body but not the mind and spirit.

- Parents get out of balance because of stress caused by questioning and doubting themselves.

- Wiser adults, including grandparents are getting out of balance because their mind is ignored. However, with age, the spirits become more balanced. Wisdom usually ensures that each body gets the proper food.

- Society tries to help by setting up schools and establishing 'rules' that all must follow. These rules don't serve the children. They don't serve the parents. They don't serve the grandparents.

What then can we do about it?

Children of tomorrow, and in some cases, of today, know that when they keep their bodies in balance they will keep their emotions in balance and their analytical skills in balance. These are bonuses to the body balance. They will have the knowledge from their soul and they will have the knowledge of their genes and physical past. They know what it is like to get out of balance. What the adults of today need to do is honor the children when they want to eat a different diet, question the 'truths' of today and their parents. They will teach your adults to question and analyze what has gone on and what was told to them in the past.

There is also a need to include grandparents in the family unit but only, and we stress only if they are willing to relate to the children as humans and not someone who should be suppressed. When grandparents or the older generation do not move forward and interact with the children, they should be kept from them and kept at a distance. This will be painful but they must be assured that they, the grandparents, are loved and all other members of the families can plant seeds to alter their ideas. If the older adults are willing, you can ask for our help and we will talk to their guides and plant seeds into their minds.

For many older adults, they are unwilling to move as fast as the world is changing. It will be difficult to keep them in balance. However, with other generations balanced, they can keep them balanced simply by being around them. We have already spoken about surrounding yourselves with humans who will help your balance. This applies to the children of the families.

Choose your schools carefully. Some teachers will move forward with the children. Others, will stay back with other generations. Should you as a human parent have to have your children exposed to these adults, it is even more important to balance the input that the children receive.

Your television is one of the worst stimulus that a child can possibly have. There are what you call videos that are OK but games and building material are best. Children can use their imagination and their mind to create what their memory tells them. This will perpetuate the memory and will also help to introduce ideas into other children and generations.

Most of all, keep the children active, listen to them and follow their example. They are truly loved ones.

Even if you are a younger soul, you can take the information of your genes, add your children's knowledge and you will be able to move forward to a higher soul age. This will prepare you for when you return to the Earth Plane again. It will also prepare you to interact with species on other planets what are already advanced.

Given the understanding and opportunities, the children of tomorrow will not have the issues of emotions that is facing children of today. Through expression of ideas, they will be able to express emotional issues in an advanced way of thinking.

You have had some writers in your past who were already advanced. These are your great literary minds. Unfortunately, their society did not allow them to be balanced and their emotions were tipped over.

Does this answer your questions?

Recently, I learned of a couple who grew up in an extremely wealthy family in Singapore. For many reasons, they fled and came to Canada with nothing but the clothes on their back. While they made a good income and gradually returned to the status they grew up in, the woman died of cancer about 10 years after coming to Canada. I asked my guides for comments on this transition in terms of lifestyle and eating. This is what was given to me.

This is an example of what not to do. While they were forced to flee and the humans did not have much time to plan, what would have been ideal was for them to follow a simple procedure.

Firstly, while still in Singapore, they should have spent at least a week eating simple foods from the country they lived in. Then a short fast before leaving to go to another country.

Secondly, once they were in the new country, another fast and then gradually introduce the new foods into their system. We have always recommended eating lightly and simple when coming off a fast. This would have helped their bodies get used to a new type of food as well as the different energy. Their bodies would never have received the old pattern of eating, even after gaining wealth in the new country.

Thirdly, the fasting would have helped their bodies heal the emotional traumas they experienced. This would have prevented the cancer from growing. She would have come to terms with the changes in their life and even when the cancer grew, she would have been in a position to break it up.

This is an example of when she should have followed all the recommendations we have given you. When the new foods were given with love and eaten with love, she would have survived, and possibly never had cancer at all.

The daughter will experience the similar trauma with her new breasts if she does not follow the fasting procedure. Again we want to say that the genes and spiritual knowledge must be integrated and this a situation where it does not appear to have happened. It will be up to the daughter to change the genetic knowledge. The spiritual knowledge has already been changed.

This passage is included in the family section because of the genetic influence on the mother and daughter. Yes, the Mother could have altered her eating pattern and survived but by **not** doing this, the trauma was transferred to the daughter and someone in the family line will have to accept the trauma that occurred to the family. It is interesting to note that when I was told this story, there was no mention of the Father. He is still living and remained healthy. This is possibly an example of the soul age and knowledge interacting with the genetic knowledge

We cannot run from who we are, not can we alter the speed of genetic changes. What we can do is acknowledge that these are facts and we can use the family and our chosen social group to work **for** us and not against.

Conclusion

Inner Bridges is only the first step and is only a small part of the overall plan of balance. There is a large quantity of information. The book stresses the need for balance, staying local, living simple and giving thanks. While **how** the individual chooses to bring his being into balance can be varied, he or she must balance all three parts — mind, body and spirit — equally. The outcome is that you will be balanced within your family, society, Earth.

Inner Bridges focuses on the philosophy and tools necessary for finding this personal balance. In many respects, it has been a book of teaching self-centeredness. However, self-centeredness has its rewards and works in many directions. Being balanced **within** the self, allows the being to share their tranquility with others **beyond** the self. Bridges work in two directions. Each time that we use a tool for balance from another realm, such as nature, we are sending back a portion of peace and contentment of our complete being.

We must realize that we are an integral part of the Earth and each contributes much to the existence of each part and the Universe as a whole This flows continuously throughout the Universe, amongst all creatures. Peace has to start within a being. Balance has to start within a being. Our Inner Bridges work within the individual, within the family, within society, within our Earth, each time moving to a larger sphere surrounding us.

You may experience confusion and a sense of awe as you start to apply the information written here. However, we recommend that you start with a small piece, practicing it regularly. Move to another piece, adding it to the first. Gradually, you succeed. This may be increasing the amount of local produce in your diet. Next you may add organic products. While these changes are happening, you may begin a meditation program. Good luck

In the later days of these channeled writings, my spirit guides started giving me additional information. I was told that this book of tools is only the first step. The second step is applying these tools to all our live and all our connections. Further steps involve deeper understanding of how we interact with all parts of life throughout the Universes. However, without the balance, peace and integrity **within** ourselves, it is difficult to work with other aspects of life.

Furthermore, we do not have to wait for further information to be given to us. Each person can apply these tools, selecting whatever works best for us, the individual. As we gain balance, we can unconsciously send it beyond ourselves into other aspects of life.

Each human being can make a big difference to society and to our world, the Earth. Many channeled writings talk about the faster vibration and changes coming to the Earth Plane around 2012. It is important that we take responsibility for ourselves and our contribution to life itself. Then, the higher vibration can only assist us and all who live on the Earth Plane.

Appendix I
Symptoms and solutions to minor imbalances

Symptoms:
Usually results from not consuming sufficient *sweet, sour* and *salty* tasting foods:
- Feeling worried, frenetic
- Low appetite
- Impulsive
- Skin is dry and itchy
- Impatient, frustrated
- Mind filled with many ideas
- Jumping from one project to another
- Feeling bloated and gaseous
- Cannot sleep
- Nervous disorders
- Constipation
- Achy joints

Solution:
- Increase the quantities of the foods that are in **list #1** with emphasis on sweet, sour and salty tasting foods, avoid cold foods whenever possible
- Eat 3 smaller meals at regular times
- Take long walks, preferably avoiding wind and cold
- Spend time in nature

Symptoms:

Usually results from not consuming sufficient *sweet, astringent* and *bitter* tasting foods:
- Angry at yourself and others
- Judgmental
- Impatient
- Skin rashes and inflammations
- Heartburn and ulcers
- Excessive hunger
- Resentment

Solution:
- Increase the quantities of the foods that are in **list #2** with emphasis on sweet, astringent and bitter tasting foods
- Eat at regular times and avoid stimulants
- Avoid hot environments. For example, take warm, not hot showers and baths. Reduce Sun bathing. Enjoy gentle breezes.
- Take time to wind down, alternating rest and work.

Symptoms:

Usually results from not consuming sufficient, *pungent, astringent* and *bitter* tasting foods:
- Lethargic
- Excessive sleeping
- Depression
- Possessive, reluctant to change

- Frequent colds and sniffles
- Diabetes, High Cholesterol, High Blood pressure
- Weight increase

Solution:
- Increase the quantities of the foods that are in **list #3** with emphasis on pungent, astringent and bitter tasting foods
- Pay extra attention to the foods, vitamins and minerals that reduce diabetes, cholesterol and high blood pressure
- Reduce consumption of sweet foods and heavy, starchy foods
- Change and alternate activities frequently
- Increase strenuous exercise
- Avoid dampness and stay warm
- Socialize frequently with friends and family

Appendix II
Food to help bring us back into balance[4]

List #1 (Sweet, Sour & Salty Foods)

General guidelines (Whenever possible, select foods that are organic from the region where you live)
- Warm food, **never** cold, moderately heavy textures
- Eat additional butter & fat while remembering cholesterol levels
- Soothing and satisfying foods
- Avoid using spices in large quantities
- Minimize all bitter and astringent foods

Vegetables
Asparagus, Beets, Carrots, Cucumber, Green beans, Okra (cooked), Onions & Garlic (not raw), Radishes, Sweet potatoes, Turnips

Grains
Oats (cooked, oatmeal cereal, not dry), Rice, Wheat

Dairy: All OK, in moderation

---

[4] Reprinted with permission from Lad, Vasant Dr., *AYURVEDA, The Science of Self-Healing*, Lotus Press, Wisconsin, 1984.

Meat
Chicken & Turkey (white meat), Seafood in general, (All in small quantities.)

Fruits (sweet, well-ripened fruit)
Apricots, Avocados, Bananas, Berries, Cherries, Coconut, Figs, Dates, Grapefruit, Stewed fruits, Lemons, Mango, Melons, Oranges, Papayas, Peaches, Pineapple, Nectarines, Plums

Herbs & Spices (All in moderation)
Allspice, Anise, Basil, Bay leaf, Caraway, Cardamom, Cilantro (green coriander), Cinnamon, Clove, Cumin, Fennel, Ginger, Licorice root, Marjoram, Mustard, Nutmeg, Oregano and Sage, Tarragon, Thyme

Oils
All oils are Good. Sesame Oil is best

Sweeteners (All acceptable)

Nuts and Seeds
All are acceptable in small quantities. Almonds are best choice

Legumes (Beans)
Chickpeas, Mung beans, Pink lentils, Tofu (in small amounts)

List #2 (Sweet, Astringent & Bitter Foods)

General guidelines (Whenever possible, select foods that are organic from the region where you live)
- **Favor:** moderately heavy textures; bitter, sweet and astringent tastes
- Cool or warm but not steaming hot foods
- Reduce amount of butter and added fat

Vegetables (Sweet & bitter vegetables)
Asparagus, Broccoli, Brussels sprouts, Cabbage, Cauliflower, Celery, Cucumber, Green beans, Leafy green vegetables, Lettuce, Mushroom, Okra, Peas, Potatoes — White & Sweet, Sprouts, Sweet peppers, Zucchini

Grains
Barley, Oats (cooked), Wheat, White rice (basmati and white)

Meat (in small quantities)
Chicken, Rabbit, Shrimp, Turkey

Sweeteners
All sweeteners OK except Honey and Molasses

Nuts and Seeds
Coconut, Pumpkin, Sunflower seeds

Fruits (All should be sweet & ripe, avoid those that come to market unripe)
Apples, Avocados, Coconut, Figs, Purple Grapes, Man-goes, Melons, Sweet Oranges, Pears, Plums, Prunes, Raisins

Dairy
Butter (unsalted) or Ghee (clarified butter), Egg Whites, Ice Cream, Milk, Cottage Cheese

Beans
Chickpeas, Mung beans, Tofu and other soybean products

Oils
Coconut, Olive, Soy, Sunflower

Herbs and Spices (Spices, generally are too heating, but some sweet, bitter & astringent ones are good--in small quantity)
Cardamom, Cilantro (green coriander), Coriander seed, Cinnamon, Dill, Fennel, Mint, Saffron, Turmeric

List #3 (Pungent, Astringent & Bitter foods)

General Guidelines (Whenever possible, select foods that are organic from the region where you live)
- **FAVOR:** Pungent, astringent, bitter tasting foods.
- Warm, light food
- Dry food, cooked without much water
- Minimum use of butter, oil and sugar
- Stimulating foods

Vegetables Generally, all are acceptable
Asparagus, Beets, Broccoli, Brussels Sprouts, Cabbage, Carrots, Cauliflower, Celery, Eggplant, Garlic, Leafy green vegetables, Lettuce, Mushrooms, Okra, Onions, Peas, Peppers, Potatoes, Radishes, Spinach, Sprouts

Fruits
Apples, Apricots, Berries, Cherries, Cranberries, Peaches, Pears, Pomegranates, Dried fruits in general

Oils
Almond, Corn, Safflower, Sunflower

Grains
Barley, Buckwheat, Corn, Millet, Oats (dry), Rice (basmati, small amount), Rye

Dairy
Skim milk, Small amounts of whole milk, Eggs (not fried or cooked with butter)

Meat
Chicken, Shrimp, Turkey (all in small amounts)

Nuts and Seeds
Sunflower & Pumpkin seeds

Herbs and Spices
All spices are good. Ginger is best for improving digestion

Sweeteners
Raw, unheated honey

Index

A

Adam and Eve, 10
Air, 17, 19
Amethyst, 168
Anger, 111
Animals, 109
Aromas, 180, 184
Arrowhead, 36
Aura, 16
Australia, 145
Ayurveda, 91, 109, 128, 140, 146, 149, 152, 164, 178, 190

B

Bach, Dr. Edward, 145
Balance, 3, 4, 8, 11, 14, 15, 18, 24, 26, 36, 37, 38, 43, 45, 46, 49, 50, 51, 53, 54, 55, 56, 57, 58, 59, 60, 61, 63, 64, 65, 66, 67, 68, 69, 70, 71, 72, 74, 75, 76, 77, 90, 91, 95, 104, 105, 108, 110, 117, 118, 123, 126, 129, 134, 139, 140, 141, 147, 149, 150, 152, 154, 155, 157, 161, 163, 165, 166, 169, 178, 189, 191, 192, 193, 197, 213
Bicycle, 192
Biofeedback, 155
Bi-polar, 152, 157
Birds, 60, 75, 76, 77, 93
Blankets, 179
Blue, 172, 174, 176
Blueberries, 136
Blue-purple, 172
Brahms, 167
Butter, 139

C

Cactus, 151
cancer, 202
Centering, 95, 104, 116
Chakra, 17, 101, 117, 142, 146, 189
Chakras, 176
Chi, 17
Chi Gong, 135, 190
Children, 9, 11, 49, 51, 52, 58, 89, 174, 177, 198
Chinese medicine, 140, 143, 152, 178
Chocolate, 130
Christians, 114, 115
Church, 26, 46
Churches, 11
Citrus, 150, 169
Cleansing foods, 126
Clouds, 79, 80, 81, 154
Color, 161, 189
Corn, 146
Corn Bread, 136
Cousens, Gabriel, 146
Cranberries, 141
Cream Cheese, 139

D

Dairy, 139
Desert, 110. See environment
Diet, 9, 12, 52, 131, 132, 134, 136, 137, 138, 139,

144, 148, 153, 157, 178, 200
Dimension, 17
DNA, 15, 163
dosha, 141

E

Earth, 6, 8, 9, 10, 12, 15, 16, 17, 19
Earth Plane, 6, 9, 10, 11, 34, 57, 81, 96, 173
Ecosystem, 117
ego, 3, 7, 8, 10, 11, 12, 22, 30, 31, 52, 99
Egyptians, 145
Elements, 19
emotions, 7, 16, 21, 31, 63, 81, 148, 161, 164, 202
energy speed, 190
Environment, 9, 11
Essence, 59, 64, 76, 83, 84, 172
Essences, 157
Exercise, 12, 15, 190
Eyes, 163

F

Family, 8, 26, 46, 67, 123, 193, 203, 204, 211
Fasting, 202
feeling, 161
Fire, 19
Flower essences, 147, 151
Foods, 15
Fruit, 129, 131, 133, 134, 146, 153, 154

G

Galaxy, 13
Garden, 43

Garden of Eden, 162
Gems, 63, 64, 82, 83, 84
Genes, 196
Genetics, 9
Grains, 132
Grandparents, 199
Grapefruit, 155
Grapes, 142
greed, 3, 6, 7, 8, 10, 11, 115
Green, 129, 142, 165, 172, 174, 189
Green Beans, 141
GROUP of 8, 5
Guides, 5
Gurudas, 155

H

Habits, 12
Hawks, 177
Healing, 11, 15
Healing Touch, 102
hearing, 161, 182
Heart Chakra, 142
Higher dimension, 9, 147, 195
Honey, 136
Hummingbirds, 176

I

Illnesses, 11
Imagination, 201
Indigenous, 162
Indigo, 168
ISHMA, 5
ISMURUS, 5

J

Jet lag, 154
Joseph, 169

K

Karma, 38, 39
koan, 102

L

Languages, 162
Lessons, 175, 195
Lifestyle, 9, 14, 61, 111, 123, 149, 184
Liquid, 129, 149, 150, 151
Listen, 194
Locale, 14
LUKE, 5, 23

M

Macrobiotics, 143, 178
Maple Syrup, 136
Massage, 148, 157
Mayan, 104, 115
Mayans, 105
meditative, 189
Melons, 131
Memory, 201
Moon, 128
mountains, 66, 74, 75
Music, 72, 73, 74

N

nature, 56, 60, 66, 69, 70, 71, 72, 73, 77, 78, 80, 82, 83, 88
Nutrients, 14
Nutrition, 12
Nuts, 132

O

Oats, 135
Olives, 130
Orange, 170, 172, 174
Oranges, 138
orchids, 61, 62
OSMOND, 6

P

Pacific Flower Essences, 172
Paths of knowledge, 196
Pepper, 143
Pets, 177
Philosophy, 21
Piano, 162
Planet, 7, 8, 10, 13, 14, 28, 49, 53, 54, 57, 58, 62, 77, 81, 86, 88, 90, 112, 115, 116, 125, 132, 148, 151, 164, 165, 168, 170
Pleiadian, 105
Politicians, 11
poverty, 7
Power, 116
Purple, 142, 172, 174, 189

Q

Quickening, 9

R

Races, 10, 11
Red, 142, 165, 172, 173, 189
Reiki, 102, 108, 117
Religion, 7, 98, 113, 114
Religions, 189
RIPPLES, 118
Rocks, 63, 82, 83, 88, 89

S

Salt, 143
Scents, 116

Schizophrenia, 152
Schools, 201
Seal, 177
Season Depression, 153
SHAY-LA, 5
Singapore, 202
smelling, 161
Smoke, 66
Society, 8, 16, 27, 32, 49, 56, 61, 76, 114, 121, 130, 197
Soul ages, 197
Spelt, 135, 142
Spiders, 166
Spirit, 3, 6, 10, 11, 12, 13, 15
Spirit guides, 10
Storage, 141
Stress, 199
Sugar, 136
Swans, 177
Swimming, 190, 192

T

Tai Chi, 190
Taste, 182
tasting, 161
Television, 201
Therapeutic Touch, 102
third dimension, 4
Transcendental Meditation, 100
Traumas, 203

U

Universal plane, 7
Universe, 3, 8, 9, 10, 11, 12, 13, 16, 17, 23, 26, 27, 28, 29, 35, 36, 38, 47, 51, 52, 59, 66, 72, 74, 90, 91, 95, 96, 110, 111, 116, 124, 151, 161, 168, 196

V

Vegetables, 135, 140, 141, 145, 151, 169, 215, 217
Vibration, 8, 9, 15, 62, 73, 83, 103, 104, 107, 110, 116, 133, 161, 162, 171, 173, 185
volcanoes, 56, 66

W

Walking, 191
Warnings, 157
Water, 19, 154
Watermelon, 131
Weather, 183
Wind, 19, 55, 57, 69, 85, 171
Worry, 194

Y

Yellow, 151, 167, 170, 172, 173
Yoga, 100, 101, 190
Yogurt, 139